Medium, Rare

A First Hand Account of Growing Up Experiencing the Paranormal

Lesley Marden

NEW FOREST
BOOKS

Concord, New Hampshire, USA

New Forest Books™

Post Office Box 2216
Concord, NH 03302-2216 USA

www.NewForestBooks.com

Well, hello there. My name is Lesley Marden and I am pretty much like every other woman in her forties out there. I am a wife and a mother of two children. I have always been involved in my children's lives, volunteering at school, acting as room parent and chaperoning pretty much every field trip that came down the pike during their elementary school years. I have never missed a chance to watch my son compete in sports and to this day, still watch as he travels with his college football team. I work hard at my job to help bring home the bacon and do everything else a typical wife and mother do on a daily basis.

As My friend Gina tells me, I am "every woman". I do not seem to stand out in a crowd, and I treat every one I meet with kindness and respect. There is only one difference between me and most of the other wives and mothers out there and this is my story. Let's just say, my life has been anything but mundane.

⚜

What constitutes a paranormal experience? Is it out of reach for some and not for others? I think that we all have the ability to experience happenings connected to the spirit world if we just slow down and take a look around. Have you ever seen a ghost? Maybe you have felt like somebody is watching you. You may have gotten a bad feeling about doing something or going somewhere that has made you change your mind. That would be noticing. The conscious act of noticing what is around you is all that needs to be done.

I have been paying attention to my surroundings for a very long time now. It is something that I have done for as far back as I can remember. As I have made my way through life's journey I have observed that most people have not had the same feelings or happenings, or noticed the little coincidences that go on from day to day. Maybe that is because I am a little different from other people.

I seem to be more aware of what is around me. There have been times in my life where I have tried to suppress and ignore the happenings around me, but I have now learned to embrace the gifts that I have been blessed with in order to help others. Within these pages are a few experiences from my life. Experiences of a person growing up with intuitive abilities.

I hope that when you are finished reading this, you will see and understand that it is okay to just be yourself. You too should embrace who you are and try to be the best person you can be. By accepting yourself, you will be able to reach out and help others, no matter what your talent or contribution to their lives may be.

My parents, Joanne and baby Lesley

When I came into this world in the mid sixties my family lived in an apartment in Mt. Vernon, NY. My earliest memories from this time are the usual type. Playing with my older sister, watching the programs of the day on TV, dragging all of my toys out and leaving them strewn about the room for my mother to pick up. But there are other memories as well that I just assumed were "normal". Instances of and memories of situations that I thought everyone experienced. What occurred to me while I was growing up I presumed were the same things that happened to everyone else. Apparently I was mistaken.

We lived in the upstairs of a brick apartment house owned by our landlord who lived downstairs. She was an elderly lady whom I remember was very nice. Back then my immediate family consisted of me, my mother and father and my older sister Joanne. As every small child experiences, my whole world revolved around my family. Of course this also included my aunts, uncles, cousins and grandparents. We were a very close knit group and would always have a family get-togethers. The gatherings would regularly take place either at my grandparent's house, my great aunt's house or at our apartment. The grown ups would always find things to do together and truly enjoyed each other's company. We were our own little community, or at least we were in my eyes. I was 3 years old.

In front of our apartment

My parents and the other grown ups would go bowling regularly. One of my favorite things about their bowling nights was knowing that they would stop at the vending machine and bring home treats for my sister and me to find tucked away in the bottoms of their bowling bags. It was almost like the feeling of waking up on Christmas morning, that excitement of knowing that there was something waiting for you to open.

One particular morning, I remember getting up and coming out of my room to sneak into the living room and discover what delectable treat my parents had brought home for me. As I made my way through the hallway, then the kitchen and the dining room, I became more and more apprehensive. I didn't want to go into the living room and open the bowling bag that was sitting directly across the room from me, in front of the fireplace, as I had done so many times in the past. I couldn't go in there while "they" were in there.

My sister and my parents were still sleeping all safe and sound in their beds but I was awake, me and "The People" in the living room. I couldn't see them with my eyes, but I knew they were there. I poked my little head through the doorway into the living room and looked both ways to check for The People. I didn't see anyone and the lure of that bowling bag was just too intense for me. I found myself running in my yellow footy pajamas, scuffling my feet across the hardwood floor as the dusky early morning light filtered through the curtained windows.

When I got to the brown bowling bag, I placed my fingers upon the black zipper and prepared to pull. As I started to unzip, knowing that my prize was just a few moments away, I was overcome by fear. Out of the blue, like a lightning bolt, I knew in my heart that The People saw that I was there and they were paying attention to me. In that very moment, I knew that I was intruding and I was not supposed to be in the living room. It was their turn to inhabit this room, and The People impressed upon me that they wanted me out NOW. They were coming closer and closer to me so I abandoned the zipper on the half opened bowling bag and made a hasty retreat through the length of the apartment to the safety of my parent's bed.

This was not the only time I had run crying to my parent's room because of them, but it is one that I can recall with great clarity and one that has stuck with me throughout my life. There were other times I knew The People were walking the floors of the apartment, but this time I was not just aware of them, they were aware of me. It is a scary thing for anyone to feel that their safety is being threatened and I think that feeling is magnified when the threat is coming from something you know is there but you can't see with your eyes.

It was a great comfort for me to know that I was safe with my parents. The People, as far as I knew, never entered the bedroom areas of our apartment. Fortunately we didn't live there for much longer. My mother. who grew up in a small country village in England, was not happy in urban setting of New York. She wanted her children to be able to play outside in the sunshine and be as safe as she was when she was a child. My parents made the decision, and moved us away from the rougher streets of Mount Vernon to the comfort of a community filled with parks, beautiful lakes and beaches. A great place for little girls to run and play safely outside in neighborhoods filled with families and children. My parents found this perfect place. We settled in a big old house in Laconia, NH.

Great Lakeport Fire 1903.
Photo credit: Lakeport Community Association

The area of Laconia we now called home, known as Lakeport, is a section of town where Lake Winnipesaukee connects with Paugus Bay and the waterway narrows and then becomes Lake Opechee. Lakeport was the site of a terrible disaster. In 1903 a large section of Lakeport burned to the ground. In our new backyard you could dig and find lots of artifacts from this time period, Broken china, old tools, metal scraps as well as other kinds of trophies. I can remember finding a dirt filled, dented thimble. What a prize! I recall scraping the dirt out of it with a twig and trying to wear it on my finger, but it was too big. I must have scraped out a little too much dirt.

In this neighborhood there are reminders to this day of the fire. There are still a few random stone foundations where the houses burned to the ground and were abandoned. I can remember sitting on a stone foundation on the corner of Fairmont St. and Belvedere St. As I sat there I could see in my head the goings on of a couple's life that had happened there before the fire. A man with hat that he took off when he entered, and a lady in a dress with an apron had lived there. I don't think they had very much money. I wondered why the kitchen I saw looked more like a workshop, with wooden plank floors and a simple wooden table with an oil lamp on it. There was also a big black iron stove with a stove pipe that climbed up the wall.

Stone foundation at the corner of Fairmont St. and Belvedere St.

I didn't pay much attention to my thoughts when they came to me like that. I would tell my mother about what I would see and she would say that I had a good imagination to think things up like that. My mom was the smartest person in the world, so I accepted her answer, and appreciated and felt proud that she thought I had a good imagination. Looking back on it now, I know that it wasn't imagination at all. The details were so clear and precise. My imagination could not be blamed for what was going on in our new house either.

I have not researched the history of my parent's house, but I do know the names of two families that had lived there in the recent years before we moved in. Before those two families, I have no idea how many families inhabited the house. I am most certain that the activity in the house is in no way associated with either of the two recent families but is most definitely associated with or attached to previous owners.

Before we moved into the house it had been altered from it's original state. Some doors had been moved and some closed up. Where there once was a fireplace, there was now a bookcase. Also, the kitchen area and mudroom had been added on and connected to the barn.

When we moved in, there was the whole downstairs, and there were three bedrooms upstairs. At the top of the stairs on the right there was a wall put up, and on the other side of this wall was a closet to an upstairs apartment. You could access the apartment by using the door on the back side of the house that also led to our kitchen. The apartment had a bedroom and a sitting room, a bathroom and a kitchen. I am pretty sure the apartment had twice been occupied. When I am up there I feel that it had once been the home of a single man, and once by a young widowed woman with a child.

I remember as we explored our new home, being very curious and crawling into all of the built in nooks and crannies. I was four when we moved in. I don't recall feeling anything out of the ordinary at first. The house was a quiet place, just a house. But before too long it became noticeable that "someone else" would come in and out of the house to visit.

I started to wake in the night and hear things and feel things. I can remember that this started happening when I was five. Our family was changing. My mother was pregnant with my little sister and my Dad was on the road for his job driving a tractor trailer across the country. To accommodate our growing family, and open up a spare bedroom for the new baby, my mother surprised my sister and me with a pretty new bedroom that we would share.

Our new sleeping quarters would be in the front bedroom with pink trellis wallpaper, and the built in shelves and drawers. On the far side of the room was the super cool sliding door on the closet, which was complete with built in shoe cubbies running up the right side. A bare light bulb in a socket hung downward with a pull chain that Joanne and I could reach if we climbed up the shoe cubbies, or on to the raised bench on the left hand side of the closet. The new twin beds all dressed in pink floral bedspreads were placed side by side, framing the big picture window. The beds were sitting on top of the new purple and pink shag rug.

My sister chose the bed closest to the wall and the closet which left me with the alternative choice of the bed with the view of the hallway and the door at the bottom of the attic stairs. I was happy with my new room and new big girl bed. I had been sleeping by myself in the little bedroom at the top of the stairs in the child size bed. I figured having my sister Joanne sleeping in the same room would be a comfort for those nights when I would wake up and listen to the noises of something that sounded like clothes rustling down the hallway. Unfortunately I did not realize that noise came from the end of the hallway which I was now on.

I was not the only one who noticed some of the strange occurrences in the house, like the strong smell of roses that would come out of nowhere in the dining room, or the creepy creaking footstep noises coming from above our heads, as if someone was walking across the upstairs kitchen floor in the apartment. It seemed everyone noticed those things. But some other occurrences in the house were apparently invisible to the other members of my family.

One night as I was sleeping soundly in my new big girl bed I was woken up because the closet light had been turned on. My sister usually fell asleep as quickly as I did each night, so I didn't think it was her. I thought maybe my mother had come in to put some clothes away while we slept. I didn't give it too much thought and turned back over and went to sleep. Later on that week it happened again, but this time my sister accused me of doing it. I told her it wasn't me. She didn't believe me. It happened again the next night, for the third time within the week. I blamed Joanne and she blamed me. I was telling her the truth. She never ever believed me. We wouldn't be able to resolve this ourselves so we ran and told our mother.

Our Mother was visibly annoyed that we were arguing. She said we had probably turned it on earlier while it was light out, and had just forgotten that we had done it ourselves, and to stop fighting about it. Neither of us believed our mother was right, but we were forced to accept her take on the situation. It is funny, but after we had acknowledged the light in the closet, it seemed to stop. It didn't happen again for quite a while. When it did turn back on, it was very infrequent and happened with no rhyme or reason.

After that incident I began to notice things that were happening during the night when the house was quiet. I would not wake up every night, in fact I slept pretty soundly on most nights. So soundly, in fact, that I would fall asleep in one position and wake up the next morning without having moved at all. I was able to slip out of my bed in the morning and have it look perfect without even making it.

On one such night of sound sleep, when my Father was home from his trucking job, I was woken up abruptly deep in the night. I could hear the sounds of footsteps downstairs. These were heavy footsteps. Heavy thud noises on the carpeting in the dining room accompanied by the sound that the china cabinet made when a heavier adult would walk through. It was the sound of plates and glasses touching together and pinging with every step. The dining room was just at the bottom of the stairs, the same room where we would smell the phantom roses.

At first I thought it might be my dad, but then I noticed I could hear him breathing in almost a snore like fashion in the room next to mine. The walking became so heavy and intense that before I realized I had left my bed, I found myself running to the safety of my parents room. I was petrified, crying and afraid that "The Man" would peek his head around the corner at the bottom of the stairs and see or hear me running and prevent me from reaching my destination.

I burst into my parents room, crying uncontrollably into the sleeves of my long flannel nightgown, trying to stifle the noise that I was making. Both of my parents sat up in bed to see what was wrong and I blurted out through my sobs "There is a man downstairs!" My father jumped up wearing only his underpants and tee shirt, and reached into his top dresser drawer. To my surprise he pulled out a handgun, of which I was totally unaware he owned, and he quickly left the room. As he exited he whispered "Stay here!" and down the stairs he went.

My mother and I sat so quietly I don't think either of us were breathing as we were trying to hear what was going on downstairs. My father returned with a look of relief, and sweat painted on his face. He told us there was no one down there and that all of the doors and windows were closed. He turned to me and said I must have been dreaming and to go back to bed.

It was definitely not a dream. I was completely awake and aware of the man downstairs. I also knew in my bones that this man was responsible for the light going on in my closet. As I reluctantly returned to my room, I noticed on my way by that the attic door was ajar. I climbed back into my bed and pulled the covers way up over my head, leaving tent like hill so I could breathe. After lying there and listening for more footsteps, with my eyes shut tightly for what seemed like an eternity, I fell back to sleep.

≈✢❦✢≈

As I mentioned earlier, I can sit in a place, like on the foundation of that burned down house, and I can see the way things used to be. This skill however wasn't always a benefit. Sometimes it would get me into trouble.

I attended an old elementary school that was just one street up from my house. It was an old brick building with lots of woodwork inside that had been highly lacquered and polished. The banisters, floors, stairs and wainscoting were a deep rich color which made the hallway with very few widows seem that much darker. I attended the Kindergarten which was housed in the basement. I liked school and it didn't take me long to make friends. I found out very quickly that my new friends only lived a stones throw away from my house and we became neighborhood playmates straight away.

On the basement level of the school, after walking down a flight of stairs, on the right was an open area with coat hooks along the wall and a room with a door on the left. This was the Kindergarten. At the back end of the open area was the boiler room. The boiler room scared me. I was always afraid that the boiler would become too hot and explode. Not only did I not like the loud seething giant metal structure in that room, but I also did not like "the man in the work shirt" who always kept busy, and in my minds eye was always carrying some sort of big tool in his hand. He wore chino type pants and a button down shirt. He was balding on top with a few random strands of hair that he combed over the baldness, and he always wore a scowl. I knew no one else could see him, because I saw him in my head. He was not aware of me, or anybody else for that matter, but I made it a point to stay away from that end of the open space and hang my coat where I could see it, closer to stairs...and the exit.

The following year I was in first grade on the first floor. Our first grade line would walk up the front stairs, in to the school, and then directly across the hallway straight into our class. My first grade teacher didn't like me much and she made no bones about letting me know it. She thought I was lazy. Well, I guess I was lazy. Even my mother would complain about that. I wasn't trying to be that way. It was just not fun doing worksheets and learning math and reading when there was so much to think about while I was in that building.

Washington Street School, Laconia, NH

I was constantly getting in trouble for day dreaming. I couldn't help myself. In mind I could see, as if I were watching a movie in my head, boys with button down shirts and wool pants and girls who always wore dresses and a teacher with bright red lipstick and a perfectly pinned up hairdo wearing what I considered to be dress up clothes. She held a long pointer made of wood in her hand. She was always making the children recite things in, the only way I can describe it, a three beat manner. On every beat she would tap the stick on the floor or in her hand. I could almost feel the vibrations under my feet when she tapped the wooden stick onto the hardwood floor. Looking back at it now I would place them in the late 1920's early 1930's. Back then I had no idea why they were wearing those types of clothes. I just took it at face value, like I would if I were watching something on TV.

Every once in a while I would get the feeling that one or more of the people from that time would actually be in the classroom or in the hallway with us, just walking through, minding their own business. I never told anyone about what I was experiencing, about what I saw going on in my head. My mother had convinced me it must be my imagination. Anyway, people would probably think I was nuts! There was one boy in particular who I would see show up more often than any of the others. He liked to just stand in the back of my classroom and watch. His dark hair was parted on the side and his untied shoes were brown leather and scuffed up. He never said anything or tried to interact.

When I graduated to Second Grade (by the skin of my teeth) I would walk everyday up the dark wooden staircase to the second floor. I always made it a point of touching the banister all the way up and all the way down the stairs. It is hard to explain, but in a way it gave me a sense of belonging. I too was becoming part of the building with all of the other people who had touched the banister and walked in the halls before me, and it was becoming part of me. The experiences that the building had been sharing with me were a part of my experiences now. The building had begun to feel like an old friend.

That year I drove my classmates insane. My family was planning a trip to England to visit my grandparents and my aunt so that they may meet my new sister Patricia. My mother hadn't been home for over 8 years and her excitement spilled over on to me.

Everyday my teacher would start the day with the Pledge of Allegiance and then open the floor in the front of the classroom for Show and Tell. My classmates would raise their hands and share about what they had done the night before, or about their plans for the upcoming weekend. Everyday I would raise my hand and my teacher would call on me last because EVERYONE in my class knew what I was going to say. The countdown to my trip to England had become so monotonous that my classmates would all sigh when my teacher finally called my name. They would all recite with me as I said "8 more days until I go to England". I can remember the look of relief on my teacher's face when I stood before the class and said "Tomorrow I am leaving for my trip to England".

Junior Pilot Wings

It was exciting landing in London, getting our Junior Pilot's wings from the BOAC stewardesses, and then stepping out into a brand new country that I had never seen before. It was all so new, yet all so familiar. The first thing I noticed was that all the people there talked differently than my family in New York. They talked differently than the people in Laconia too. Although my mother is English, I never really heard her accent. She just spoke to me like my mommy. It kind of took me aback seeing a 3 year old speaking with an English accent. I thought to myself "Wow, what a smart little kid being able to talk like that!"

The next thing I can recall that really stuck out to me was how OLD everything seemed. Not old in the sense how a little kid looks at a 50 year old, but a feeling of how this place is not anywhere near as new as my country is.

We arrived at my grandmother and grandfather's house in a little village of Emneth. It was very much different from any apartment or house or building I had ever been in before. First off, there was a strawberry patch that was bigger than what I would consider a garden. Rows and rows and rows right in their yard! The front door faced the road but we went into the door at the back of the residence because it was more accessible from where we parked the car. That car with the steering wheel that was on the wrong side.

The back door brought us into a small kitchen area with a white sink, an old fashioned white oven and a small refrigerator. That led into the room where we spent most of our time. It had a table and chairs for eating and a few comfy chairs for sitting and a fireplace where instead of burning wood they would burn coal. After exiting that room, there was a hallway that led to the front door and the staircase.

On the way to the front door was a front room on the left. Immediately I knew that I did not like that room at all. I would not go in there without someone else with me, even during daylight hours. If I was in there with someone else I would not stay long at all. I was just six turning seven, but I knew that this was not a space that welcomed me. I did not see any "people" and the whole situation just felt different from any I had experienced before.

At night when we had to pass that room to go to bed, or heaven forbid, I had to go to the bathroom which was upstairs by myself, I was in a full out run going past that door. I remember feeling that there were no people walking the floor in there as they did in the apartment in Mount Vernon. I do remember thinking that there was a swirling stream of energy like a breezy whirlwind that you couldn't see or feel with your eyes or with your body. It was definitely not a warm and fuzzy, welcoming you received from the energy, but more of a stay out of here, no trespassing type feeling. I chose to heed the message.

The upstairs housed two bedrooms and a bathroom. The bathroom had the best toilet a little girl could ever use. The tank was high up on the wall and it had a pull chain to flush. Every time I pulled the chain I thought of Lurch from the Aadams Family and imagined the grand sound of a gong. I couldn't resist saying in my deepest voice possible "You rang?" with every flush.

Down the hall was a bedroom that Joanne and I shared. It was very cold in there all the time. So cold, that when we turned down the blankets to get in to bed, you could feel the cold radiating off from the bottom sheet and mattress. My grandmother offered to put hot bricks in the bottom bed or get some electric blankets but my mother told her we didn't need such things. Our bodies would warm up the blankets quickly enough. I was a little put out that she said that, but she was right. We soon warmed up the beds and we would fall asleep quickly.

I did not feel uncomfortable in the bedroom, but it again it did not feel normal, it just felt different. The house itself wasn't extremely old but the land it was built on seemed to be. I know that sounds silly because the earth is an old place. To better explain, I guess what I am trying to say is the land that the house was on had been used or occupied by other structures and people before my grandparent's house was there. That pretty much sums up the feeling I got when we visited London as well.

The thing I remember most about London is not Buckingham Palace or the changing of the guards or even Big Ben. The one place that impressed me the most was Kings Cross Railway Station. For years and years ahead I would have dreams about it. There is some sort of energy in the area where you climb aboard the trains. I remember looking up at the colors of the glass in the ceiling and just soaking it in, as I was being dragged by the tight grasp of my mother's hand, through the grand structure of iron and bricks. I wanted to stay there and just be in the deep pool of feelings I was experiencing. I felt happy there. I felt like I had been there before and that left a lasting impression.

That memory had faded over the years but were all brought rushing back recently when I visited London. As soon as I walked out of the station and onto the loading platform under the colored glass it all came back to me like being reunited with an and old friend. I had a permanent grin as I reentered the energetic place. I was so moved I felt the need to take a picture of the ceiling so I could keep it with me always.

King's Cross Railway Station, London, England

Walking around London with my parents for me was not like walking around New York City. The sounds of traffic and the smell of bus fumes were similar and the people passing you on the streets was similar, but the energy was totally different. Walking around NYC, I would look up and marvel at the huge tall multi story buildings and sometimes think of Irish policemen and scruffy boys with wool pants and caps. In London I would look at the buildings and the movies in my head would just flip on and one movie would be interrupted by another as we passed different places. Men in white wigs was a common theme of the movies as we walked past the structures that they belonged in.

I also saw important men and fancy ladies that rode around in carriages being pulled by horses. Tall dark hats for the fancy men and pretty adorned hats for the ladies. There would be smelly looking people as well in my movies, but somehow the smelly people never seemed to talk to the fancy people. The smelly people always seemed to belong outside while the fancy people belonged in the buildings. I remember wondering where the smelly people lived.

The hustle and bustle of the city was all but forgotten when we left London and journeyed back to the quiet villages of and countryside of Cambridgeshire. The movies in my head had never been as plentiful as they were In London. On our car rides, I do recall passing churches and seeing mental movies of burials and priests with old weathered ladies walking with old weathered men, and passing random houses and thinking that they were haunted by former owners.

There was one particular house we passed. It sat back from the road a bit, which allowed a good long look at it. I noticed that the window in the front downstairs corner of the house looked different and I couldn't take my eyes off it. All of the other windows had curtains, but this window was just gray on the inside. I could feel a strange fascination with the house and it scared me.

As we drove past my mother said "Look, at that that house. Do you notice how the window looks funny." and pointed at the house. She said "Oh, that is the house where they had a room that was so haunted that things would literally fly around in it. Even though the owners kept the door shut tight, they didn't feel safe. They decided the only way they could continue to live in the house was to pour cement to the very top room and turn it into a solid block. Even after they had done that they still heard noises coming from it." I thought to myself, why would anyone want to live there.

Our time in England seemed to fly by and had come to an end and it was time to return to the States. After we had landed in Boston it struck me that I had become used to the feeling of England. The stark contrast I was able to discern was again apparent in comparing the two countries. It was nice to be back home but I missed the adventure that had unfolded in my head. Things were quickly back to normal with being back at school. All of my classmates were relieved that my family was not planning on taking anymore trips to England for a very long time.

⁂

A new family had moved to Laconia and there was a new girl in school. She and her family were also from New York. There were two second grade classes at my school, and she was placed in the other class so I would only see her on the playground. As luck would have it her mother met my mother at a local Nursery Guild meeting and became friends. It was fate that Denise and I would become best friends.

Denise's mom could drive, my mother couldn't. My mother had a fear of driving so she never learned. To have a new friend with a driver's license was a definite plus for my mother. Before, Joanne, my mother and I would walk to the closest market and bring our Radio Flyer wagon to roll the groceries, and Patricia back home in. Mom did a lot of walking back and forth from the market in those days with my father on the road and all. Ellen was more than happy to bring us to the local market once a week. My mother and her three kids piled into Ellen's car with her three kids and we all managed to fit in with room to spare. One day after shopping, Ellen invited my mom over for coffee.

I recall that first time I stepped into my new friend's house which was exactly one half mile up the street from my house. It was also directly across the street from our new school that we had graduated to when we entered third grade.

The house itself felt stark although there was furniture in it. Despite the furnishings, it felt as if it wasn't a home, it was just a shell. There was a sense of uneasiness that came along with the tour of the house. I noticed the echoes in the rooms and the empty feeling I got when I walked around. The emptiness and hollow sounds of Denise's house seemed to disappear after a while as the family settled into their home and made it their own.

I started to spend a lot of time there with Denise as we played together. Her mom would stop at our house almost everyday after she got out of work. She found a job as a medical secretary at the hospital. My mother was a stay at home mom so she enjoyed seeing Ellen every afternoon, drinking coffee and hearing about what was going on with the people about town.

My mom then agreed to take Denise and her two brothers at our house in the mornings before school so Ellen could be at work for 7am and not worry about leaving her kids alone. Other things were changing at home as well. My father found a new job in town as a machinist and my mother was expecting another baby. All of a sudden it seemed like our lives had gotten much busier and just started cruising along one day after another.

Soon my brother was born and days seemed to fly by. In our house the wall to the upstairs apartment was knocked down to make access to another bedroom and my father started to tear apart the living room to make it less like two rooms at the front of the house and more like one big one.

It was now an everyday occurrence that Denise and I would be together. We were pretty much together all the time and she would regularly invite me to her house during the day and sometimes to sleep over at night. Almost every trip to Denise's house would bring forth some feeling of uneasiness and depending on the day or the time of day would determine the level of that discomfort.

I am just going to put it out there and say that Denise's house is haunted. Flat out haunted. There is a higher level of interaction factored in for me to label a place to be "haunted". I noticed as we would play outside that the house seemed to be watching us. It seemed to watch you with it's window eyes. It was actually not the house, it was "her", The Lady.

Denise's House

The Lady would always let me know that she was there. Some afternoons Denise would invite me to her house after school and then I would be invited to stay for dinner. Things would be going along just great and then I could feel this sort of oppressive atmosphere take over the entire house. This would usually happen shortly after nightfall. I knew The Lady had come to watch us. She was okay with the family living in her house and it was almost like she had accepted them and was protective of the children. Even though I was a child myself, she let made me feel that I was an outsider. The house belonged to her and I should not overstay my welcome. I was certainly welcomed by the family, but not by her.

She was a stern older lady with a staunch strictness about her. She liked things her way and she could enforce her rules upon me by intimidation. She knew I could sense her and she would present herself to me in my head. I could see her in my mind's eye with her arms crossed and gray hair that was pulled up into a tight bun. I also could see her black dress with a pin tucked yoke and a cameo just under the collar that stood up about an inch all the way around her neck. Her sleeves were close fitting and the shoulders were gathered and ever so slightly puffed. She would make herself know to me in the day as well as the night. More than one of my night's sleep had been interrupted by her in that house.

When I would sleep over we would set up a cot pushed up right next to Denise's bed. My cot was about a foot lower than the top mattress of her bed. One of the reasons Denise and I got along so well was because we share a great sense of humor. We could keep each other laughing and amused for hours. We always had fun together. This night had been no exception. We giggled and talked and were silly until her mother called up and told us to go to sleep. We said goodnight to each other and I drifted off into a very deep sleep.

The next thing I knew, I was awoken with sudden and absolute terror. There stood The Lady at the foot of my cot with her arms crossed and a mean stern look on her face. She was angry! This time she was not in my head, she was actually standing in the room inches away from me almost completely outlined by the light that was coming through the cracked open door to the hallway. I acted upon instinct and did the only thing that I could. As if I were on auto pilot, I threw my body toward the top of Denise's bed, grabbing the glow in the dark rosary beads that she kept on her bedpost and retreated as fast as lightning into my sleeping bag. I covered up my head and curled up with my knees under my chin to get my feet as far away from the bottom of the cot as I possibly could.

I was too scared to cry as I clutched the beads that were emitting a very dim soft green glow. I prayed to God himself to come and save me. I honestly felt that she would try to do me some sort of bodily injury if I had left myself exposed to her. The heat from my rapid breath being trapped underneath the shelter of my sleeping bag soon made it harder for me to breathe. I thought I may suffocate as I prayed and held the beads in my hands and pressed the glowing crucifix to my forehead. I felt her leave the room.

She had done what she had set out to do. That was to remind me that Denise and her family might live there for the time being, but that house belonged to her. She made the rules and my sleeping over was not to her liking. I held those beads for the rest of the night and kept the sleeping bag over my face, positioning my mouth close to the zipper that was done up as far as it could go, so I could get fresh air without actually having to expose my head to possible danger.

She would interrupt other guests in the night who slept over in the house as well. She was aware that I had the ability to sense her and that she could intimidate me by showing herself and impressing her wants and feelings upon me. For other guests who were not sensitive and were sleeping without a family member in their room she would repeatedly keep turning on the light to interrupt their slumber.

To this very day when I pass that house I always look to the upstairs windows and into the big picture window on the front to see if she is watching. I still have dreams about Denise's house. I am most certain that The Lady is still there.

⚜

I absolutely love the fact that in the next instance of a brush with paranormal activity there are witnesses. Most of my experiences happen psychically, within my head or through means of intuition, but this one was seen by not only me, but my sister, my cousins and my aunt as well.

It was Christmas break from school and our family had traveled to New York to our visit relatives for the New Year's Eve festivities. We all gathered at my grandmother's house in Mount Vernon. Aunts and uncles and cousins were all crowded around the dining room table. The adults were all talking and laughing and leaving us kids unattended and bored. Joanne was 12, I was 10, my cousin Jay was 10 and my cousin Michael was 8. Now keep in mind this was the 70's and we were in a somewhat quiet neighborhood so the parents did not mind if we ventured within shouting distance of the house.

We all bundled up in our coats and told the adults we were going to take a walk to the church which was about a block away. Saint Paul's Church is a lovely old church that is also registered as a national historic site. On the church grounds is a graveyard where many or the area's Revolutionary War soldiers are buried. Even though it was late December, there was not a lot of snow on the ground. The night before it had snowed maybe an inch and a half. Not enough to play in and not the type of snow that was good for snow balls. It was enough though to make snow angels in, and enough for my mean older sister to scoop up and throw in my face.

St. Paul's Church, Mt. Vernon, NY

When we reached the edge of the graveyard we noticed something strange. The snow was virtually undisturbed so what we witnessed stuck out like a sore thumb. What we saw looked to us like Foghorn Leghorn, the big rooster from the Looney Tunes cartoon, had been walking through the cemetery. These two-toed foot prints were somewhere just over 2 feet long and looked to be made by one thing walking around. Even stranger was where the footprints walked. They walked directly through the family vaults as if there were no walls to them. Half a footprint would lead through and be cut off by the cement and stone wall and would again appear coming out of the other side.

We were scared. Here it was about 10 o'clock in the morning and we couldn't have been more spooked if it were midnight on Halloween. We ran as fast as we could back to my grandmother's house and told the adults that were sitting around the table what we had seen. Like my mother always thought of everything out of the ordinary I would tell her, all of the other adults seemed to think were letting our imaginations get the best of us.

Stubbornly, to prove we weren't lying, we convinced our Aunt Eloise (who was in her very early twenties) to come down to the graveyard and just take a look. She had begrudgingly agreed to come with us. All four of us were dragging her and talking all at once about what we had seen and how she wouldn't believe her eyes and how it was up to her to convince the other adults that we weren't lying. As soon as we got close enough to be able to see what we were so eager to get back to we all stopped dead in our tracks, too scared to go any further.

Her jaw dropped as she took in what we had told her she would witness. It didn't take her long to say "Oh my God, let's get out of here!" You didn't have to tell us twice, we all turned tail and started running back to my grandmother's house.

Family Vaults, Burial Ground at St. Paul's Church

Looking back as an adult on this, I would better describe the tracks as a very large cloven foot. If you know anything about the paranormal, this is not a good thing to find. A footprint of this kind may have been left behind by something less than friendly. Some thing that may have been demonic. It is hard for me to give any guess as to what it may have been. I have never been back to the church since. Although I am curious as to what may have been walking through that graveyard, I have no intentions of ever trying to encounter something of that nature.

⚜

All of these childhood recollections are true. They are factual and they happened to me and left indelible marks on my life's path. I carry them around with me in my backpack of experience. There are so many little things in there as well. Small occurrences that I have had happen to me all of my life. I have experienced coincidences that a lot of us share. For example, thinking about a person, then turning a corner and they are standing there or singing a song in my head and then turning on the radio and that song is playing or thinking about calling someone and the phone rings.

I have a pretty good knack for knowing what will arrive in the mail before the mailman gets to my house. I have also had colorful dreams of places that I have never been and in my travels, stumbled upon them and known what would be around the next corner. When I was in high school I met a boy whom I knew I would marry. His name was Mike.

I can remember vividly knowing the details of my future as I was on stage during a skit that some class members and I were putting on for our senior class day. I did not have a big part in the skit. My part was to sit at a desk and act disinterested in what was going on at the front of our fictional classroom. After having played a lead role in our Drama Club's production of Bye, Bye, Birdie, this was a piece of cake. No lines to memorize, no singing, no real actions or stage directions to follow.

You would think that being on stage in front of the student body and faculty members would be a little nerve wracking for a teenager. Strangely it wasn't. The skit started and I had my notebook and pen and I was playing my massive role by sitting at a desk and doodling in my notebook. The stage lights were bright and I could not really see anyone or make out any faces in the darkened auditorium.

As I looked down at my notebook, my surroundings seemed to fade away and I started to write things that would eventually come true years later. I wrote down my husband's full name and my full married name as if by some unseen hand had taken over mine. The information I was writing I could also hear in my head.

I would have two children. A boy, his exact full name was written out onto my paper, and a girl whose first name was missing, represented by an underline, then her middle and last name was printed out onto my notebook page. I also saw in my head that my future husband was wearing a uniform with a badge which I then interpreted as a policeman and I was a teacher. "A teacher?" I thought. I always said as I was growing up that I would be a nurse.

With that original thought I was sucked back into the reality of what was going on around me and I realized that I was on stage in the middle of our skit. Had I seen the future or was this just "daydreaming" again? At this point in my life I was beginning to figure out that maybe my daydreams were just a bit more that what my mother called my imagination. I was now sixteen and there were stranger things happening than ever before.

※◎※

The Man in my house was becoming active again. He was making noises and strange occurrences were common. The wall that separated the apartment from the upstairs had been taken down, which opened up another bedroom which my parents moved into, and a newly refurbished bathroom for us to use. The sitting room of the apartment had been made into a dressing room for my parents, but was now being used as Jimmy's bedroom. The upstairs kitchen was just the same, but the appliances had been taken out and the door to it always remained shut.

I was sixteen, Joanne was eighteen and my little sister Tricia and brother Jimmy were 10 and 8. My mother now had a full time job and was gone all day. Joanne was never home but when she was we did not get along, creating drama and yelling and fighting. My father was still working at the machine shop but by now was promoted to Vice President in charge of Sales. His second job was keeping the local barstool occupied. Let's just say my father was not a happy drunk, which also created a great amount of discord in our home.

It was apparent that energies were being stirred up in the house. It was not a very happy place to be anymore. It was almost like The Man was feeding off of the energy, making him stronger. I could feel him lurking around the house. He was all over the house, not just in the dining room. I could sense him in the upstairs hallway and strangely this would coincide with the attic door. It would always be ajar no matter how many times it had been shut. If there was a strange happening in the house we would go and check to see if the door was open...it was.

Attic door ajar

My bedroom was no longer at the end of the hall by the attic door. I was now in the bedroom my parents occupied when we first had moved in, which was directly at the top of the stairs and to the right. From my bedroom door I could look straight through the new hallway created by the renovations, past my parents new room on the left, then straight through the door that was used for both the bathroom and then Jimmy's room.

View after renovation from my bedroom

New noises were being heard in the house. My mother had heard a cowbell ringing in the barn and she was hearing the rustling noises passing her doorway at night, one night She thought our two Black Labs had come upstairs and run past her door. They hadn't. They were sleeping soundly in the kitchen. My little sister was awoken one morning when she heard a man's voice telling her to get up because she had slept through her alarm. My little brother would sometimes climb into my bed just to be with somebody. The footsteps in the upstairs kitchen continued.

The man was walking the house at night and it was a common occurrence for me to feel as if I was being watched as I tried to fall asleep. It became a habit for me to stay up until I could barely keep my eyes open, drag myself upstairs and climb into bed so I would fall asleep quickly. On this particular night I did just that. I crawled into my bed and seemed to fall asleep almost immediately. As I turned over later in the night, I had woken up enough to realize that the house was still, but I was not alone.

As I rolled over I opened my eyes. I was shocked into being fully awake. My wits seemed to shoot straight out of the top of my head as I came to realize that floating above me was a man. I could see his face and his shoulders directly over mine. He was hovering at less than an arms length above me and was staring at me. He did not look menacing in the least, but kind and meaning no harm.

He had brown hair and a round face with slight jowls. I was more than stunned to see him floating there. My heart started pumping to the point where I thought it would burst through my chest. I closed my eyes and turned over and tried to breathe normally in a lame attempt to make him think that I wasn't aware, or wasn't bothered that he was there. I remember thinking as I pulled the covers up over my head in a nonchalant way "Pretend he is not there and he will go away, pretend he is not there and he will go away."

I was scared, but not in the same way I had been scared by The Lady in my friend's house. I knew in my bones this man would not harm me. I almost think he was there to check in on me. As I feigned sleeping, I could feel him back off and go away. I wondered how many times he had done that in the past, and if he would ever do it again. Thankfully, for my heart and blood pressure, that was the one and only time it ever happened.

The following morning I told my family what I had experienced. I likened his round, slightly jowly face to Benny Hill's. I described everything exactly how it unfolded. My family all laughed at me and called me a liar. My mother told me to stop telling such ridiculous stories. It hurt me deeply that my account of what had actually happened had been so easily dismissed. I usually kept what happened to me to myself, because no one ever believed me anyway, but I felt that this was a major incident and had to be told. After the reaction that I received from my family that morning, I had made up my mind. That was that day that I vowed to myself that I would never tell my family or anyone about my experiences ever again.

❧

I decided to just try to shut out what was happening around me. I started drinking with my friends and I found a sort of comfort by numbing myself with alcohol. I finished High School and took a year off to decide what I really wanted to do with my life. I had no direction. I only wanted to have a good time. Mike went into the Army and I was taking a math course two nights a week at the Community College. I worked during the day in a supermarket bakeshop.

All of my friends had started their journeys and had begun their lives. They had gone off to college or into the military and I was left behind. I quickly found new friends who were Seniors at the High School in the neighboring town, some of whom I worked with at the store. We all shared a common interest, we all liked to drink. I cut off all of my long brown hair that had grown down past my waist to a short bob that was cut just above my chin and dyed it blonde with hydrogen peroxide. I hadn't been eating and my 5 foot 10 inch frame was now down to 139 lbs. It was almost as if I was trying to become another person, searching for a new identity.

As I immersed myself into partying every night, and as I did, my father was making lifestyle changes as well. He had finally come to terms with his alcoholism and quit his great paying Vice President's position at the machine shop and entered a rehab facility.

I hated my father when he was drunk. He was never home when he was sober. I don't think he was ever really sober. I hated everything about him, and yet I was doing to myself the very thing I hated most about him. I was drinking to excess, just like my dad.

I applied to Plymouth State College to fill the need of having some sort of direction in my life. I waited and waited for a letter to come from the school. The day it did come, I was too busy to notice.

I had been at work from 6am to noon, had run home at lunch to shower off the muffin mix and yeasty bread dough from my morning baking, glammed myself up to look nice as I stood behind the bakery counter until 3pm, made plans with my friends after work to go to a party, ran home to freshen up, then out the door to illegally purchase a 12 pack of beer for my drinking pleasure and off to the party.

I didn't get home until after 1am. Since I hadn't eaten for a day and a half, I immediately headed to the kitchen to look for some food. My letter was waiting for me on the refrigerator, stuck to the front of the freezer door. I opened my letter but couldn't read it. I was too inebriated to keep my eyes focused on the words. I forgot about the food and brought the letter to bed with me. When I woke up the next day I read it with bleary eyes. I had been accepted.

I entered college as an Elementary Education major with a minor in Special Ed. I found that college was a fantastic place for a girl who liked to party. During one night of partying in my second semester, I met a new boyfriend. He was fun to be with and the attraction was undeniable.

In my second year I moved out of the dorms and into an apartment that I shared with my him and he quickly became my fiancé. I pretended that things were great, but I was so unhappy. I truly loved my new fiancé but knew in my heart that he was not "the one". We connected on a very deep level and had an all encompassing passionate relationship, but the down side to that fire was that we would fight terribly. My mother absolutely hated him and she was barely civil to me. My weight ballooned.

On one seemingly normal day I attended my class in the early afternoon and had an hour before my next class. I decided to go to the college library, which was something I rarely, if ever did. For no reason in particular I decided to pick up a copy of my hometown newspaper. I perused the front page and then opened the paper up to the obituaries. I was shocked. There screaming off the page was a familiar name. Mike's mother was dead.

I hadn't seen Mike in so long, and my life had changed so much in the time that he had been gone. I was a little more than apprehensive to show up at his mother's wake. I had no clothes that fit me. I borrowed a dress from a friend at school.

My Fiancé drove me to the wake and waited for me in the car. Mike invited us to his parent's house with some other friends afterward. It was nice to see the people from high school that had shown up at Mike's house, and after the initial introduction of my new boyfriend and with a beer in my belly, the tension eased a bit. Mike was not very nice to me as I sat next to my fiancé drinking my beer. He would randomly moo at me, but even through his attempt to be hurtful, I could feel the connection we had was still there.

After the funeral, Mike went back to Germany and I resumed my unhappy life back at my apartment. A few months passed and my fiancé and I continued to fight and I continued to gain weight. We couldn't afford to buy beer all the time anymore. We didn't have enough money to eat on a daily basis either.

Sitting sober, hungry and alone in my apartment I heard a voice. This voice was not in the room with me and it didn't come from outside. It was in my head. It said to me in an authoritative manner, "It is time to move on". I knew it to be true. I thought to myself "Did I think that or was it spoken to me?" I wasn't sure, but I listened. I broke off my engagement and I moved home.

My mother was relieved that I did not get married and continued to complain about my now ex-fiancé on a daily basis. I was more miserable than ever. Months passed and I managed to still make my way out with friends to drink and party regularly. I dated but with no serious intentions. Then Mike came home.

⚜

I was now 22 and Mike and I had married and were expecting our first child. I already knew it would be a boy and what his name would be with out asking the doctor to tell me the gender. My son Chris was born weighing 10 lbs 14 oz. The universe surely works in mysterious ways. I had been abusing my body with alcohol and now I had been given a reason to stop. As soon as I was aware of my pregnancy my drinking ceased. After my son was born I would drink socially on a Saturday night with friends, but not at all like the fish that I had been. My focus was now on my family.

Mike was working in a local grocery store, a member of the National Guard and a member of the Fire Department's Call Company. With the absence of alcohol in my system, I noticed that I was again able to sense things.

I used to get these feelings that my husband and I would refer to as "fire willies". We would be doing something banal where there was not much to engage the mind, like driving in the car somewhere. I would say "There is going to be a fire, I have a willy." and sure enough within 24 hours or so his pager would go off and he would be summoned to a fire.

One night I had awoken from a dead sleep. Something wasn't right. I checked on the baby and he was fine, but I wasn't. I started pacing around the downstairs of our duplex apartment, looking for something that might be causing my distress. I called up the stairs to Mike "Has your pager gone off yet?" Within moments Mike's pager went off sounding multiple alarms. The local lumberyard had been turned into a blazing inferno at the hands of an arsonist. Storage buildings filled with beautiful lumber were shooting flames high into the night sky.

Mike jumped out of bed and into his turnout gear, swearing with every movement he made. In an adrenaline rush, he flew down the stairs and out the door. It wasn't very far from where we lived so I bundled up the baby and put him in the stroller and we walked to the chaotic scene and sat on the step of the newspaper building with many of my other neighbors and marveled at how high the flames reached up and how much heat the fire was giving off from where we were sitting.

Mike and the other men that were on his hose were credited with saving a building that night that was filled with more lumber. He suffered steam burns through his turnout gear and the truck they were pumping from sustained damage from the intensity of the heat from being so close to the flames.

As I stood there with the other people who were watching, I knew that the abilities that I had been suppressing were still with me and I should just accept them. I didn't have to let other people know. I would just keep them to myself. I bet my boss at the time wishes that I could have been the only one to experience what happened to us a few weeks later.

❧⛯☙

I was working in a fast food restaurant as an assistant manager. I loved the fast pace during the rush of lunch and dinner, and I loved the quiet times when the staff could joke and laugh. One night, after closing, my manager asked if I would help him with the month end paperwork. He and I checked all of the doors making sure they were locked and we settled in as the last staff member was leaving after clocking out. The employee left the building through an exit only door that automatically locked behind him.

The office was located in the kitchen area and had a large window that overlooked the grilling and sandwich areas where the workers would be positioned during hours of operation. All was quiet but the sounds of the calculator and our muttering of numbers.

All of a sudden there was the sound of heavy footsteps, that we could also feel reverberating through the wooden support beams of the structure. Someone was running through the length of the dining room. The quickly paced thudding noises became louder, and the vibrations in the floor became more pronounced with every sprinting step closer.

Something ran through the kitchen door, without opening it, and ran past the front of our large office window and continued down through sandwich assembly areas to the complete opposite end of the building where the freezers, refrigerators and the electrical panel that controlled the lights and the time clock were.

Both my manager and I instinctively looked to the window as the sprinter would be passing, but there was no one. The kitchen door did not swing open and there was no "body" accompanying the sounds we heard. My manager looked at me, with every bit of color now drained from his face and said "Uh, that's enough for tonight, why don't you go get the lights."

He stuffed the papers we were working on into his briefcase as I made my way toward the end of the building where the footsteps would have ended up. (So much for chivalry!) I clocked out and turned off the lights. I intuitively knew what had just happened had not been caused by something that would hurt me or even acknowledge me.

As I made my way back to the office to get my coat and keys, I saw my manager's break lights leaving the parking lot. I had to go lock the door he fled though and make sure the restaurant was secure before leaving myself. He never stayed later than his employees after that night and soon put in a transfer to another restaurant that was closer to his home....I wonder why?

Not very long after that, I had another child. Wouldn't you know, it was a girl, 11lbs 15oz. I was surrounded by my family as I sat in my hospital bed with my new baby desperately trying to pick out the perfect first name, as I already knew that her middle and last were already set in stone. Name after name was offered as a suggestion as I looked down at this new child who was as big as a three month old. As soon as I heard the name Rachel spoken, I knew in my heart it was hers.

⁂

An opportunity for us to buy my husband's childhood home was presented to us as Mike's father was no longer able to make his monthly mortgage payment. We offered to assume his mortgage and therefore, assume ownership of the house.

Unfortunately Mike's father had let his house fall into a terrible state of disrepair. Being young and foolish and not knowing that my husband had inherited his father's lack of handyman skills, I thought "We can just fix it up!" I thought all men could fix things...silly me! Almost every window was broken, there were holes in the walls, painted over wallpaper peeling off the walls, half assed fix jobs and dirt, dirt, dirt in every room. We had our work cut out for us.

Mike's family helped us move in and after they left Mike went straight upstairs to go to bed. I said that I at least wanted to get the kitchen cleaned before I turned in. Although this statement was true, the deeper truth was that I did NOT want to go upstairs.

I could feel the presence of a spirit who was not happy at the top of the stairs. I was not about to climb those stairs or even go anywhere near the bottom of them where I might be able to see him, or even worse, he might be able to see me. I felt he might throw something at me or he would be able to shove me down the stairs if I attempted to climb them. I made myself busy in the kitchen scrubbing the years of dirty Mop 'n Glo layers from the floor. When I was too exhausted to go any further I slept with one eye open on the couch.

In the morning after finishing up in the kitchen, I decided my next project should be my bedroom. I had already scrubbed the back bedroom which was now the kid's room before Mike's dad had moved out so they were already sleeping in a sterilized room. I couldn't believe the years of neglect in this house that were apparently now my responsibility. I grabbed a clean bucket of disinfectant and water, a scrub brush, some rags and a mop and headed upstairs.

My bedroom during daylight hours did not seem the least bit intimidating. I noticed a crucifix hanging on the door frame of my bedroom closet. As soon as I laid my eyes upon it I knew that it had been put there for a reason. That was the first thing I cleaned in that room. I felt that cleaning Jesus was a priority (It still hangs there today). Although I wasn't intimidated by being upstairs, I felt like I was being watched.

Crucifix above my closet door

To make my cleaning experience more tolerable I decided to plug in the stereo. Anyone who knows me can tell you that I am a Queen fanatic. I absolutely love their music and of course had to put in a Queen cassette tape to play while I worked.

As I was scrubbing down the walls and woodwork, I was singing at the top of my lungs to the blaring stereo across the room. The tape abruptly stopped. My immediate thought was "Aw, I hope the tape isn't tangled up." but when I got to the stereo I was stunned to see that the stop button was pushed in. I pushed the play, rewind, fast forward and the eject buttons but the stop button would not pop out. I stood up and said out loud "Okay, I'm sorry, I won't play my music anymore." Nothing happened as I stood listening to the faint echoes of my voice bouncing off the empty room's walls. I then said, more emphatically, "I promise!" With that, the stop button popped back out.

I removed the cassette from the tape deck and placed it on the turntable's dust cover. Although this house was now my responsibility, I was sharing it with a former owner. I have kept my promise. Freddie Mercury's voice has not been allowed to fill the airspace of my bedroom since.

A few evenings after that day, we invited some friends over. The children were sleeping in their room and we were all downstairs. There were five of us all together. Mike and two friends were in the kitchen and I was with a friend in the living room.

As we sat talking to each other from either side of the room, a sound came from directly above us. It sounded like a heavy chest was being dragged across the floor of my bedroom. I looked at my friend. He looked at the ceiling and said "Did you hear that?" and started to chuckle. As his focus came back to my face I said to him "Don't laugh, I have to sleep up there!"

As we started our life in this new house, Mike was starting a new job. He was hired by the Department of Corrections as a Corrections Officer. (Hmmm, wearing a blue shirt and badge...) He was working 2nd shift in the prison which was located about 30 minutes away. He would leave at 2 o'clock in the afternoon and return home at about 11:30 at night. I had gotten quite used to his new schedule. I would feed the kids, give them a bath and get them to bed at about 7. Then I would settle in for some peace and quiet.

I was soon introduced to the random slamming of an unseen door in the house. I could never exactly pinpoint which door was being slammed but it was near the back of the house. When it did slam, it would do so with such a force that it could be felt throughout the entire structure, rattling the windows and making the walls and the floors shake.

The first couple of times it happened I was a little freaked out. It would usually happen late at night, just before midnight but I have also heard it in the wee hours of the morning as well. On occasion I would think to myself "Huh, I haven't heard the slam tonight." as it wouldn't happen every night. It was and still is a common occurrence though.

My bedroom seemed to be the center of activity. I would try to wait up for Mike to get home but sometimes I would just be too tired. I would reluctantly go up to my bedroom and sleep with the light on. I would pretend that I left it on for Mike's sake. Even with the light on I could feel someone watching me from the closet area. I would try to remember to close the closet door before I got into bed but some nights I would forget. Once I was under my covers and warm and comfortable I would not get back up to close it.

One night I was lying there waiting for sleep to take over as the closet watched me and I felt the cat jump up onto my bed and start walking around. As he made his way up the bed toward my head, I put my hand out to pet and welcome him, so he would stay and keep me company. I anticipated the feeling of his warm fur brush my hand. As the cat walked past my fingers, I couldn't feel him. I realized the cat wasn't there so I opened my eyes. I remembered putting my cat outside before I went to bed. I sat up and looked around. There was no cat, but there were indents on the comforter when one had just been.

Another night soon after that one I had gone to bed and had remembered to close the closet door. It was soon time for my husband to be home and we had had a disagreement so I wasn't looking forward to his arrival. He was becoming intolerably full of himself and I didn't like the way he was acting at all.

I laid on my bed with my eyes closed, on my side facing the windows with the light on, thinking about how could I go on being married to this pompous jerk that he had become. I felt someone sit on my bed by my shins on my side of the bed. I was startled but knew straight away that I shouldn't be afraid.

This was a kind and gentle, nurturing soul. She stroked my thigh as if to tell me that things will work out and that she sympathized with me. Then she was gone. I didn't know who she was but she obviously had my best interest at heart and wouldn't hurt me. I was definitely startled by this and held my breath when I felt her sit down, but when she had gone, I felt comforted.

It was at that moment that a little light bulb went of in my head. I realized that the things that had happened to me all of my life may not be normal for everyone, but they were normal for me. I had a new feeling of acceptance for these things and I didn't need to be scared of them anymore. I accepted that I coexist on this planet with these spirits.

These things, these experiences were all real. They are a part of who I am. I started to pay attention a little more closely and not wait for things to happen to me. I started to actively look.

⚜

Unfortunately things for Mike and me had gone south. I took the kids and my dog and lived with my parents for a while. Needing a job now I reentered the work force after being at home with my children since Rachel was born. Rachel was now in Kindergarten and Chris was in Second Grade. I got a part time job in a restaurant as a hostess at the bottom of the street that my parents lived on so I could walk to and from work. It felt good to have some independence and be able to talk to other adults for a change.

My kids stayed in the bedroom at the base of the attic stairs and I was back in the first room I ever had directly at the top of the stairs. The kids were uncomfortable at bed time so I would lay down with them until they fell asleep. I would wait for The Man to show, but he didn't. I wanted to acknowledge him, but I didn't get a chance. The house was very quiet during our stay.

The time Mike and I spent apart had opened up his eyes to many things and he made some very positive changes in his life by seeking out counselling. It took several months for me to decide to go back to him. He did not realize how much he valued what he had until it was gone. He was a totally changed man. No longer full of himself and willing to see what his actions and behaviors had done to his family. I had a newly found respect for him to make such enormous strides to get his family back.

⁂

After we had moved back in and had gotten back into the routine of our life at home, I became more and more involved with my children's school. I soon took on room parent responsibilities and went on every field trip that came down the pike. I especially enjoyed the historic field trips. I hated history when I was in school. I thought it was boring. Well, were my eyes opened in a big way.

A few of them stand out in my memory, as I am sure they do for the other chaperones that were in attendance. Not because of the fantastic history lesson that was being taught in such a way that you could touch it, but because of that one parent that lagged a bit behind the group, with her hands at her sides, her fingers splayed, and a look of concentration on her otherwise blankly staring face. Yup, that would be me. It was apparently obvious on two trips in particular.

The USS Constitution, Old Ironsides sits on the shores of Charlestown, MA as a grand trophy of american history. As we approached the fine ship, I was immediately drawn to her majestic presence. I marveled at her masts and was glad it wasn't my job to climb them to the top or sit in the crows nest.

As we boarded I knew that my experience was already much more fantastic than the 5th graders that were making their way up the gangway to receive their history lesson. I hadn't had movies in my head as vivid as these since I was a little girl looking at the streets and buildings of London.

Immediately in my head I was seeing men in impressive uniforms, with white pants and fitted coats with tails standing about and other men not dressed nearly so impressively scurrying about carrying barrels on their shoulders, moving massive ropes and cleaning.

Unfortunately I missed most of what the nice man at the front of the group said as he led a discussion about the ship to our class. I gathered that he had been talking about dates and times and the uses of the boat while I was watching the vivid images in my head. I secretly hoped he didn't call on me to answer any questions.

We went down below deck and there was a spirit in the sleeping quarters where the hammocks would hang. I couldn't see him with my eyes, but in my head. He was aware of my being able to see him as I noticed he was staring at me. He smiled at me so I smiled back. As I did, a parent said to me "What are you smiling at?" I looked at her and said "Can you feel them?" "Feel what?" she said. "The ghosts on this ship." I replied. She laughingly said "No" and walked on.

At that moment, I didn't care that other people might think of me as strange. I was so in the moment and enjoying the sights and the sounds and smells that I was experiencing. I continued to do my thing as we toured the rest of the ship. I noticed that other parents and staff were taking note of me walking cautiously around the lower decks, going into other areas that were of no interest to the group and running my fingers along the surfaces that were near me.

I wasn't actually focusing my eyes on the objects around me because I was looking at the images in my head. I must have looked odd just standing there with my back to the crowd looking at the floor. I decided that I was okay with that.

This happened again on another field trip. This one was at Shaker Village in Canterbury, NH. The Shakers were a group of people that would only take in orphaned children. They were not allowed to have relationships with each other as they viewed each other as brothers and sisters. The men and women had separate entrances to buildings and they made separation a key throughout their day. Since there were no babies being born the Shakers eventually died out and left behind a beautiful reminder of their craftsmanship and lives. Their land and buildings stand to this day as a museum. A museum that has spirits mulling about.

Shaker Village, Canterbury, NH

Again I was lagging behind the group on the field trip. We were not allowed to touch the artifacts they left behind and I fought the urge to break the rules. I so wanted to touch every thing I put my eyes on. The built in storage spaces were impeccable. Beautiful closets, drawers, and shelving, all built right into the walls, kept the houses and their lives uncluttered. Spinning wheels, irons, stoves and well made chairs were all set out on display as well as tools and other everyday things they would use.

As we walked around the beautiful grounds and buildings on the compound, I was keenly aware that some of the brothers and sisters remained, doing their chores in the gardens and in the buildings. The men were wearing brimmed straw hats and the ladies white linen caps with string ties under their chins and long dark dresses as they went about their business. The building's rooms were filled with sunshine and there was a warm inviting feeling about. The hallways were shadowy and the floorboards creaked and they echoed as we walked. I had the distinct feeling that this warm and comfortable space during the day would turn into a very creepy place to be at night.

The same parent that spoke to me about smiling on Old Ironsides noticed my hand splaying behavior as I walked behind the children. She asked if I was sensing spirits again. I looked her in the straight in the eyes and with a smile on my face answered her. "Yes, there are two older women here. They are doing chores. One is putting away laundry and one is cleaning with a rag." I thought she might laugh again, but she didn't. She could tell that I was not lying to her. She smiled at me and said "That is really cool."

Shaker Village, Canterbury, NH

❧❦❧

There are other "field trips" so to speak that I have been on where I have had some amazing encounters. One of them being our family vacation. Being young parents, Mike and I experienced some pretty severe financial hardships. Once Mike started working for the prison, and I started working a hostess, our finances were still tight, but nowhere near as grim as they once were. We had a few dollars we could spare and we decided to take our first family vacation. We decided to head south toward warmer climates for our children's April vacation. The kids had 9 days off and Mike is very much into military history so I mapped out our route and made reservations for our hotel stops. We climbed into the mini van and we were off.

Our first stop was Washington DC. We jumped out of the van for a few hours and walked The Mall. For us, this was instant spring. We left our home in Laconia where it was cold and there was snow on the ground. In DC, the cherry blossoms were in bloom and it was a good 30 degrees warmer than it was in New Hampshire. It wasn't the jolliest of stops, as the kids had just spent 8 hours in the car sleeping on and off after leaving our home at 2am, but it was well worth the effort. After taking in the US Capitol Building and all of the monuments on the mall we jumped back into the van and were off to our next destination.

Williamsburg, Virginia is a beautiful, beautiful area. I highly recommend this as a fabulous family destination filled with history and fun for everyone. Colonial Williamsburg is a fascinating place with it's streets and buildings and historical value in abundance. Some of the buildings we entered had no effect on me whatsoever, but there were a few in particular where my senses were at their peak. One of these was the Peyton Randolph House.

Peyton Randolph House, Williamsburg, VA

The Peyton Randolph House is a large brown structure and as I entered I knew immediately that there was spirit activity inside. Although the tour guide told us that this house belonged to the Speaker of the Virginia House of Burgesses leading up to the Revolutionary War, I was immediately aware of a very strong willed woman.

She was a prominent force within this house. I believe she ran a tight ship and was in charge of all goings on within the household, including the children. She impressed upon me that if she were absent, the house would fall into utter chaos. She was tremendously self important. I found myself taking pictures left and right, hoping to catch something on film. I was that convinced that she was there and I wanted to prove it. She made herself known to me in almost every room in the house.

With these impressions and thoughts going through my head of this particular spirit's characteristics and mannerisms, I realized that with this experience I was receiving much more, in depth information than I had received in the past. The tour of the house went by very quickly, or it seemed to. I wanted to stay a bit longer and see what other information would be put in my head, but it was time for another group to go through.

We left and headed across the parade field toward the Magazine area where the guns and ammunition was housed. As we walked, my husband and I stopped dead in our tracks and we looked at each other. I asked "Did you feel that too?" and he replied "Every hair on my entire body just stood up on end as we walked across that patch of grass!" I smiled broadly as I was glad that somebody was finally having the same experience that I was having and I was able to share it. We both turned around and walked across the same piece of earth where we both had felt the energy that effected our bodies in the same manner. No luck, it was gone. I believe we both had walked through, and come in contact with, a spirit energy. That moment in time is one that I will remember, and one my husband will never forget.

From Williamsburg we traveled on to Gettysburg, PA. Holy Cannoli! Before we even drove into town, I was starting to feel energies. There was a long stretch of road that led into town, flanked on either side by farmland and rolling hills. Now, as I mentioned earlier, I never paid attention in my history classes because I thought it was boring. Well, if I had ever imagined myself being swept back in time as my thoughts were racing and the movies in my head were showing me, I would have been the best history student known to man!

The movies and the drama and the emotions that were filling my senses were like nothing I had ever experienced. As we walked along the battlefields I could smell gunpowder and blood and musky dirty body odor. I could hear shouting and crying and fighting and silence all at the same time. I realized as I was walking, I was doing so in the same manner as I had on Old Ironsides, cautiously, with my fingers splayed at my sides.

I was aware that I was being watched by a tired dirty man whose bearded face was worn and weary. He was sitting by a tree. I could see him sitting there in my mind's eye. His sad eyes were such a pale shade of blue that they stood our against the dirty skin that surrounded them. He wore a blue uniform and had crossed swords on his hat. He didn't have one of those little billed caps. This was a larger hat with a brim all the way around. He was so sad.

His sadness stays with me as I remember him, just sitting there, feeling empty and alone. He watched me as I passed him, as he had watched others who had walked by him before. He was aware of my knowing he was there and I felt badly about that. I wanted to give him a hug. I had no words for him. I was at a loss, and so was he. I left him sad and lonely as he watched me leave.

I had gotten used to keeping images like his bottled up tightly inside of me. I had become very good at putting my life into neat little compartments. When my dad was drinking, I kept him and my life at home in a little box inside my brain and ignored that part of my life while I was at school. I would do the same with these fantastic experiences from Gettysburg and Williamsburg, keeping them in a nice little cubby inside of me while I was busy being a mommy and when I was working.

≈°◎∾

My sister Joanne bought a big old colonial home with her husband in Strafford, NH. It was large and beautiful. It had a fireplace in the kitchen as well as the dining room and the master bedroom. It had post and beam ceilings and original stenciling on the living room walls. Outside it had a huge barn and an orchard of fruit trees and grapes.

I was excited to help her move in and we made arrangements to meet up on her first morning there at 6am to get an early start on cleaning and moving furniture. Her husband was still in North Carolina finishing up his job there.

When I arrived Joanne invited me in. Although there were boxes piled up everywhere, my first impression of the house was like stepping back in time to simpler days. It was warm in the kitchen and I remember thinking to myself how lucky she was to be living in such a charming place. I did not stay long though as my sister was not well at all. Her first night in her new home was not as she had hoped. She had a fever and had not slept well. She thanked me for coming over and I left so she could go back to bed.

As anyone who knows my sister could tell you, Joanne is a bit of a cleaning freak. She is in her glory when she is scrubbing and disinfecting her home, and the skin off of her knuckles. It did not take her long to set up her new house and make it shine. But there was something about this house that was different. Although she had placed all of her belongings into this spotless beautiful house, it would never really belong to her or her husband. A former owner was still in residence.

Almost immediately after moving in Joanne began telling stories of the happenings in her house. While lying in bed at night, she would hear banging on the floor, as if someone were holding a wooden pole in an upright position and would lift it up then bop it onto the floor. She described how it would take hours for it to slowly make it's way across the room.

She also made claims that parts of her house would become freezing cold for no reason and at the same time she would feel as if she were being watched. The feelings and the cold would disappear as quickly as they came. There was also the tale of the front bedroom upstairs, that no matter how many times she would scrub it, the room would continue to smell like an old man.

Then there was the upstairs bedroom that protruded off of the original structure of the house and was supported by stilts. That room just gave Joanne the creeps. I found this information puzzling, because when I stepped into the house that first day, I found it to be inviting.

Room on stilts, Joanne's house, Strafford, NH

Joanne invited me, my mother and one of my mother's friends from where my mom worked to come over one night and use a communication tool that my mother's friend had. When we arrived, Joanne had a lovely fire warming up the kitchen and it was very cozy. We all sat around her kitchen table that she had placed in close proximity of the fireplace. I positioned myself close to the divine warmth that the fire provided and my mother's friend sat next to me.

This woman fascinated me. When I looked into her eyes, I could tell that she could see things and had knowledge beyond that of normal people. The tool she brought with her was a Psychic Circle.

She explained that this communication board was not dark like a Ouija Board. To use the Psychic Circle you have to open up with a prayer of protection, and when you are done you would do the same by closing with a prayer. The Psychic Circle has many symbols as well as the alphabet printed on it's colorful board. One must keep one hand on the flat glass planchette while the other hand is kept on one of the elemental symbols located at the corners of the board.

The rimmed glass disk under our fingertips moved with ease and precision and brought forth much information. It told us that the house had a dual purpose in it's early days as it was a private residence but also a public building. It also gave us information about the private family cemetery across the road. At one point during our session as we sat next to a gorgeous fire, the room became cold and the atmosphere seemed to change. It felt very uncomfortable and stark. Just as quickly as the oppressive feelings appeared, they dissolved and were gone.

Private Family Cemetery, across the street from Joanne's House

After having that experience, it didn't take my sister long before she ran out and bought her own Psychic Circle. I purchased one as well but I didn't like to use mine. I felt too responsible for the people who were sitting around the board. Joanne would invite me over to use hers, and I was okay with that.

One day, while my kids were at school, Joanne had invited me over for a visit. As we were drinking coffee she asked if I would have a go at the Psychic Circle with her. I agreed and we settled in. We said our opening prayer, and soon the glass disk was scooting across the board. As we were asking questions, a spirit who referred to itself as "The Old One" was giving us answers.

Suddenly, out of nowhere, as Joanne was asking The Old One questions, something in my brain "clicked". As Joanne was forming the questions with her words, I already had the answers in my head. I was astonished as the glass disk spelled out the very words that were inside of me.

I looked at Joanne as she asked the next question, and I spoke the answer out loud before she was finished asking and before it was spelled out on the board. This was a first for me and I could not understand how it was happening. How could I have the answers to questions of subjects I had no knowledge of?

I looked at the clock and I realized that I would be late picking up my kids from school. We closed our session with a prayer. I left my sister's house and began my trek back to Laconia. As I was driving I heard a voice in my head. The voice said "Now, Remember what happened to Eloise".

A few years before, my Aunt Eloise was driving her car on a New York parkway when a spider dropped down in front of her. She freaked out and lost control of her car. She crashed through a guardrail and her car came to a stop on the grass. Luckily, she and her young son were not hurt. What puzzled the officials at the scene, was the pattern of the skid marks that were left in the roadway. The rubber marks were clearly heading straight toward the part of the guardrail that would hold cars back from falling off the bridge that she was on and into the deep ravine below. As if her car had been pushed by some unseen force, the skid marks took a sharp unnatural change in direction and she miraculously was somehow guided to the grass instead of the ravine.

A few seconds passed and a spider dropped down in front of my face from my car's visor. I did not panic because I had been forewarned. Someone was definitely looking out for my welfare.

⚜

Joanne and her husband only lived in that house for a few short years. The decided that it was too much house for just the two of them and decided to move closer to Ferd's work. Before they moved out my sister invited my kids and I to spend the night. Mike was at National Guard training and Ferd was hiking with some friends in the White Mountains.

It was a lovely evening filled with games and snacks. We all enjoyed our evening and, as always, had fun being together. The time had come to call it a night, so the kids and I retired to the futon in the living room. I did not sleep very well, being flanked on either side by my children. I kept waking up every time one of them moved. I figured if I stayed as motionless as possible, their bodies would lie still.

It was just after 2 am. I had heard the clock chime about five minutes before, when I was aware of a man standing in the doorway. I did not open my eyes to look at him, but I could see in my head that he stood about 5 feet eleven inches tall and had longer brown hair that he had pulled back.

He was wearing pants that went to just below his knees and had a button down shirt. I am sure that he was aware of us lying there an had come to check out the situation. He was the head of the household, this was his house. He was not there to disturb us, and left a few minutes later.

The next morning I told my sister about the man. I didn't want her to make fun of me as she had in the past when I had told her and my family of the things I had experienced, so I told her that I saw him in my dream. I knew it wasn't a dream, but I couldn't face being laughed at again.

⁂

The day came for Joanne to pack up her belongings to move out. Ferd was working and I offered to help her. I dropped my children off at school and made my way to Strafford. We were both busy pulling her kitchen wares from the cabinets and placing them securely into labeled boxes.

It was around 10:30 in the morning. The sun was shining brightly outside. I was reaching into a deep cabinet underneath the counter to pull out the pots and pans when I was overcome by cold. I had never felt such a uneasy discomfort in all of my days. I stopped what I was doing and I said to my sister "Oh my God, there is something behind me." It seemed that the atmosphere around me had changed and was now sickeningly oppressive. I no longer noticed the sun shining. I felt as if the room had become dim around me. I was scared, genuinely frightened. I said "Joanne, I don't like this." She replied "I get creeped out sometimes too. Just ignore it and it will go away."

I don't think she was aware of the level of intensity that I was now experiencing. This was not the gentleman who visited in the doorway of the living room. I do not know "what" it was. I do know that it was not nice and had bad intentions. I do not believe this energy belonged to the house, but was there before the house was built and was not human.

Originally I was saddened to hear that my sister would be moving out of this beautiful old Colonial home. After having had this brush with this, this entity, I was glad she and her husband would not be sticking around for this "thing" to reappear and possibly harm them.

~୬◉୬~

Working in a restaurant, you meet quite a variety of people. Some people I believe you just meet randomly, and some you meet on purpose. A new waitress came to work at the restaurant. She was a middle aged mother who needed to make some extra money to get her son through college. Her name was Janet.

I believe she was placed in my life by divine intervention. Not only did Janet know almost everyone who came through the door to eat, but she also knew members of my family. She told me she knew my dad because he used to play softball with her husband. She knew Joanne because they had both worked at the Laconia State School.

Janet is one of the kindest people I know and she always has everyone's best interest at heart. It is no wonder that one Friday afternoon, when she came into work, she said to me "Do I have a job for you! There is an opening at the school I work at for a one to one aide, for a little girl with special needs, and you would be perfect for it." I personally wasn't looking for another job. The one I had provided me with food money for the week, and Mike's job paid all of the household bills. I told Janet I would look into it. Janet worked full time as a secretary to the Principal at Woodland Heights Elementary School. When our shift ended, and Janet was leaving for the night she said " I will see you at school when you come in to apply!" I agreed that I would come, we said goodnight and she left.

I honestly thought about going, but was on the fence about committing myself to a full time job. If I did take on this new position, I wouldn't be able to volunteer in my children's classes at their school. I had become accustomed to being able to run up the street with something that my kids had forgotten to take to school, and walking them home in the afternoons. Was I ready to let them become more independent? I think I was a little bit afraid that they would find out that they didn't need their mommy as much as their mommy needed them.

The week flew by and it was Friday again. I showed up for work at the restaurant as usual and was setting up the work stations into sections for the waitresses when Janet came to the hostess stand with her hands on her hips. "Are you going to apply for that job or what! I already told the Principal you would be coming in to apply and that you would be perfect." I didn't want to make a liar out of my friend, so that Monday, I called and went in for an interview. I was hired that day as a One to One Aide for a little girl in 4th Grade.

I had no idea how fulfilling my new job would be, I not only worked with my student, but with two other special needs students as well. Everything in my life seemed to fit seamlessly together. This new and wonderful job gave me an opportunity to fill my need to help other people. Teaching and supporting the growth of the children somehow warmed my heart. I was also so touched by the way the other students in the class embraced and encouraged my special needs students.

As I spent more time with my assigned student, I began to notice a skill within me begin to emerge. My student had some very severe health issues. I noticed on the days she was feeling poorly, I knew it right away.

Not only by the way she was acting, but because I knew it in my head. On some days I could even feel her ailments. I always knew when my own children were sick, but I chalked that up to a mother's intuition. Was I just forming a close bond with this child and thinking of her as one of my own? I wasn't sure.

I followed this child and the other two students up to, and throughout their 5th Grade year. I had come to really love my new job and was saddened by the news that since my student was leaving , my job at Woodland Heights would no longer be available.

It wasn't until mid summer that I found out that I would again have a job at Woodland Heights, but only part time. There was a Kindergarten student arriving in the fall who would need one to one assistance. I still had my restaurant job, so this was great. Just before school started in the fall, I received another phone call. It was from another elementary school across town who also had a Kindergarten student who needed assistance. I would work at Elm Street School for the AM Kindergarten session, and at Woodland Heights for the PM session. This time, both of my students would be boys, and I again had a full time job.

I loved Kindergarten! The children were so sweet and fun, and I got to sing and dance and help the children express themselves creatively while they soaked in the curriculum. Working in the upper elementary grades, you get mentally exhausted. In the primary grades, you become physically exhausted. It was a nice change though, and I found that I honestly loved each and every student.

When children are first introduced to a public school environment, their little bodies are not accustomed to the plethora of germs that are lurking on all of the toys and tools in the classroom. Therefore they get sick easily. I was noticing while I was at school, I would have very frequent headaches and other slight ailments that would be uncomfortable, but not enough to say "I'm sick".

The curious thing about this was as soon as I left the building I would feel better. I did not quite understand why this would happen, so I started to drink lots of water, thinking it may just be dehydration. Nothing seemed to help. Some days I would feel fine, and other days I just felt yucky. I knew as soon as my day was over I would be fine, so I just accepted it.

When the Kindergarten year came to a close I was given the option to choose the child I wanted to follow to First Grade. I chose to stay with my afternoon student at my original school, Woodland Heights.

Over the years my job has changed. I moved from a One to One Aide position to a Classroom Assistant, received my Level II Para Educator Certification from the State of NH, and I am now working with Special Education students in multiple grade levels.

As the years passed, I noticed that I could focus in on which students felt ill. Not by their actions, or how they looked, but by my ability to feel their ailments, as if they were my own. I knew instinctively that their illness did not belong to me because it was just impressed upon me. I liken the experience to a husband who is having sympathy pains when his wife goes into labor. Sometimes the symptoms I feel are more intense than others, but they always pass.

My sister Patricia was thinking about what she could give my mother for Christmas that would really mean a lot to her. She came up with the idea to give my Mom her frequent flyer miles so that she may go back to England to visit with her sister. One of the best parts of that present she gave to my mom was that the frequent flyer miles also included an extra person could fly free.

My mother asked me if I would go with her because my Father had to stay home and go to work and take care of the dogs. Luckily I was able to get the few extra days off from work and go during a scheduled school vacation. This would only be my third trip to England. The first trip was in Second Grade and the following trip would be when my Grandfather passed away when I was in Seventh Grade.

When we arrived it felt just the same as it always had, old. My uncle Roy and auntie Chris were at the airport waiting for us. They drove us from London to their home in Outwell, in Cambridgeshire. I love my aunt's house and it felt good to be back and to be with my auntie, uncle and to visit with my cousins again.

My aunt asked me where I would like to go while my Mom and I stayed with them. For no reason, out of the blue, the words "I would love to see Edinburgh" came out of my mouth. I had seen on the Travel Channel about Mr. Boots who haunted the underground vaults and tunnels. Maybe that is why I had said what I did, but I wasn't sure. Being the best aunt and uncle in the world, they granted me my request and we were off to Scotland.

Luckily for me, my uncle loves to drive and he loves Scotland. We drove up the major highway to Edinburgh, so there wasn't much scenery to be had. We passed a lot of what looked to be nuclear power plants that could be seen off in the distance from the roadway.

Then we came to the beautiful shoreline. The rocky coastline jutted out into the sea, and not too much further was Edinburgh. Our first stop was Edinburgh Castle. It was well into the evening so it was closed. I didn't care. I jumped out of the car and ran over to the main door and touched it. I was in awe of how old it felt. I wondered how many hands had touched it before mine had.

I turned around and noticed the view. You could see the ocean and a large bridge. I ran to the edge of the car lot and looked over the wall, and as I looked out over the city I became very calm. I looked at this magnificent place through eyes that had never seen it before, but I knew, somehow, that I had seen it before. I remember thinking how odd that was. We drove around a bit then looked for some lodging.

We found a hotel, checked in, and then we hit the street. My mother told me there was a tour of the underground vaults and we should go catch one. You didn't have to tell me twice!

There was a man in a cape and he was announcing that he had tickets to the tunnels. I think he was an actor, or an older theatre student. He handed us our tickets and told us that it was getting dark, and that our group would be the last to go down into the tunnels. He said he doesn't like being down there any later than he had to be.

He took us around the streets and into a courtyard. It was where the public executions would be held. I felt absolutely nothing as he told us the history of the area we were in. He took us around the corner where there once was a cemetery that had flooded and all of the bodies were sticking out of the ground. Again I felt nothing. I felt no spirits looking at me or letting me know that they were there at all. There were no movies going on inside my head either. I wondered if this tour was fact or fiction.

It had gotten dark. I noticed that it was past 9pm and the darkness of night was still not complete in the Scottish sky. Back home it would have been dark by 7pm at the latest. It was time for our group to go down into the tunnels. My uncle didn't want to go at first because he doesn't like ghostly stuff. He did decide to go with us, but he made sure he wasn't last in the line. I was.

As we made our way down the stairway it didn't seem creepy at all. The stairwell was well lit and there was a door at the bottom of it. We filed through the door one by one. As soon as my foot crossed the thresh hold, I knew for certain that this tour was for real. Instantly without a doubt I was aware of dwellers.

The people I was seeing in my head were very reminiscent of the dirty people I had seen in my movies as a little girl on the streets of London. I was aware of children as well big smelly menacing men. There were a few women down there as well as we passed the brick cubbies. One of these women had children with her, and the two other women I think were prostitutes. There were also sounds in my head of men down there doing metal work like blacksmithing or something. After we passed the "cubby area, things in my head quieted down.

We had entered a dark empty hallway area and came upon arched rooms. The tour guide was speaking but I wasn't listening to his words. I was walking around, just like I had on the school field trips, not paying attention, but in my own little world, with my fingers splayed at my sides. I could feel an energy, but I was not aware of any beings. I couldn't put my finger on what it was that was going on.

Our tour guide led us into the arched vaults and we were able to go inside them and move around them on our own. I was wondering if I would be able to encounter the infamous Mr. Boots, as I ran my hands along the bricks in the archways. My uncle looked at me and seemed a bit uncomfortable. I smiled at him and kept on my way.

I must lose all track of time, because just like that, the tour of the vaults was over. The tour guide seemed like he didn't want do be down there any longer than he had to be. I did not get to encounter Mr. Boots after all. We went back up to street side and the tour brought us into the supposed haunted alley ways across the street.

When we arrived I was distracted by a person in our group who thought, since we were outside, it would be okay stand in the middle of all of us and smoke. He lit a cigarette and blew the smoke up into the air. As I watched the smoke curl in the air as it drifted skyward, my attention was shifted to one of the small doorways in the alley. I thought for certain, when I looked over at the doorway with my eyes, there would be a skinny malnourished looking man standing there, but there wasn't.

I could see him standing there in my mind. He was sick, he was sad, and he looked cold and lonely. He had big dark circles underneath each eye. I could feel that his lungs and chest hurt. There was no doubt in my mind that this man had died of Pneumonia. The doorway he was standing in was now a door to an apartment. I wondered if the tenants ever noticed him standing there or if he ever went inside.

I moved to another door way on the opposite side of the alleyway. There were lights on inside. I could tell that not so nice things had taken place in this alleyway. Fights, skirmishes, crimes...and with that thought, the tour had ended. It was time to leave. I didn't want to go yet, things were getting interesting. But we hadn't eaten yet. We found a lovely restaurant to dine at and then retired to our hotel. I was so tired and full from dinner that as soon as my head hit the pillow I was out.

The next morning my mother and I walked down to the hotel restaurant where we were to meet my aunt and uncle. Once there we were greeted by a very handsome young man. I smiled and said good morning and when he opened his mouth, I couldn't understand a single word that came out. I did the thing I usually do when I have no clue, I nodded and smiled, and then I grabbed my mother's arm and held her close to my side. I whispered into her ear "Don't you dare leave my side." and she burst out laughing.

An interesting thing about the Scots, they cook everything in oil, even breakfast. Eggs, in oil. Bacon, in oil. I couldn't believe it. I must say though, breakfast was delicious. As soon as we were all done we were off to discover the beautiful Scottish countryside.

My uncle and my mother had a discussion of where we would like to go next. My mother said that I would probably enjoy a trip to the Roman Bathhouses. My dear uncle mapped out a route that went straight down through the middle of the country.

We traveled along small, meandering back country roads. The roads were so narrow that I was afraid we would meet up with a car coming from the other direction, and there would be no room to pass. In all of the many, many miles of country road, this only happened twice! It was the most breathtakingly beautiful countryside I have ever seen. We were lucky enough to happen upon a foal in a group of wild horses who had just been born and was standing up for the first time on very wobbly legs. There were so many sheep I wished I had just a penny for every one I had seen.

We came to a ruined castle where we could stretch our legs and my uncle could take a little catnap. The castle was a little farther than my mother wanted to walk, so my aunt told me to go ahead and she and my mother would keep each other company. I jumped over the closed gate and started walking.

Crichton Castle, Near the village of Crichton, Midlothian, Scotland

As I was walking I noticed how the clouds made shadows that danced upon the abundance of rolling hills, as if they were hopping for one to the other. I don't exactly know what came over me at the very moment, but I started to cry. I was so overwhelmingly happy that I couldn't contain my tears. This caught me quite off guard. I wasn't expecting a reaction like that at all. I felt like I was finally home and I never, ever wanted to leave.

Once I had wiped the tears from my eyes and I climbed up what was once a moat, but was now a very steep inconvenience, and made my way to the castle. I was surprised to see a man in a car at the entrance. The gate was closed, I remembered climbing over it. I entered the castle and started looking around. The man followed me in and charged me money and gave me a pamphlet of information. He stayed in his office as I poked around all of the fantastic nooks and crannies this structure had to offer.

Parts of the castle were intact, and some of it was in ruin. As I was in a long corridor, I could hear in my head a man yelling to someone down the hall, and his voice echoing off of the walls. I believed this man to be the owner of the castle. Then, as I stood by the giant gate that allowed access to the inner area where it was open to the elements, and looked up toward the sky. As I did I was aware of busy men who took care of horses doing chores and gathering buckets of water and shoveling horse droppings.

Courtyard wall, Crichton Castle

I soon could hear from off in the distance my mother and my aunt yelling my name. I made my way to the front of the castle and thanked the man. He chuckled as he listened to the two ladies yelling my name as if they thought I had fallen to my death and they were coming to save me.

At the Scotland/England border we stopped the car. It was overcast but the gray skies couldn't distract from the beauty of the landscape. We were very high up and I was in awe of the scenery that lay before me. I will always keep that memory with me, as well as the feeling that I was leaving the one place in the world I truly belonged.

Back at home in the States, I looked at my pictures of my trip to Scotland often. What an adventure I had, being in the underground vaults, touring the countryside, visiting castles and traveling without a care in the world. With my children now being teenagers, and being more independent, I took a good long look at my life and my level of happiness.

I am a happy person by nature, but this trip made me aware that I felt there was something missing. On this trip I felt like I was alive. It made me realize that everything I did was for someone else. My parents, my children, my husband. Everyone around me seemed to be doing things that they enjoyed and I decided it was time for me to get out there and do something I liked. I tried a couple of crafty projects, I took time out to read, I even started running...make that jogging...really slow jogging. Nothing seemed to fill that empty space inside of me that needed to be nurtured.

One day while I was searching aimlessly on the internet, I stumbled across an internet radio show that piqued my interest. The title of it was Ghost Chronicles with Ron Kolek and Maureen Wood. I tuned in, and in no time, I became a faithful listener. I looked forward to the show every week. Months passed quickly, and every week I would be sitting there listening to the hosts banter back and forth on various topics in the paranormal.

I had joined MySpace, mainly to keep an eye on my children's interactions with their friends and their online behavior. Lo and behold, can you guess who friended me? By some random act of the internet gods, I had a friend request from Ghost Chronicles. How could that be? Did they know that I was listening to their show? I had never logged into the chat room. Was it fate or a random coincidence, I didn't know. I accepted the friendship and tooled around the MySpace page that actually belonged to Ron Kolek.

I found a link to The New England Ghost Project's website. The NEGP is a professional ghost hunting group which Ron Kolek founded and Maureen Wood is his fantastically talented Trance Medium. On the website was an advertisement for an upcoming ghost hunt that they were hosting and the public was invited to attend. It was a tour of New England Haunted Lighthouses and the fee included lunch and bus fare. They also had some well known psychics scheduled to appear. Now, that sounded like something I would enjoy. I signed up immediately then left a message on Mr. Kolek's page saying that I would be attending his ghost hunt and I would see him there.

I was really looking forward to being with people who understood what I had experienced all of my life. That ghosts and spirits were real and they do interact with people. I really got excited about the trip. I was about to do something just for me, something that I felt I was meant to do. Maybe I could go out into the world and use my ability that had been bestowed upon me, and use it purposefully.

I was so excited the day of the trip, I could hardly contain myself. My mother was a little put out that I had not invited her to come with me. She thought I would need someone to sit with, and to talk to on my trip. I reminded her that I am a big girl, that I am definitely not shy, and that I can make friends easily. I didn't need anyone to hold my hand. What I told her was true, but really, I wanted to go by myself. This was about me.

The trip started out at a bus stop in Portsmouth, NH. It was a gray day and it looked as if it was going to start raining at any moment. When I arrived there was a group already waiting.

As I approached, I wondered if any of the attendees were there for the same reasons I was.

There were a few older couples, mother and daughter teams, and a man who seemed to be there on his own, as I was. He had come very well prepared for a ghost hunt. He had a book to be signed by one of the special guests, a camera around his neck, and a multi pocketed belt on his waist that contained different gadgets. He had an EMF (Electro Magnetic Frequency) meter and a point and shoot digital thermometer that you see the ghost hunting teams use on the television shows as well as a few other goodies.

A nice bearded man with glasses approached us. He introduced himself and started checking us in and as he did, handed us information about the places we were going to visit and the itinerary of the day ahead. His name was Jeremy D'Entremont, and I liked him instantly.

Some people approached from down the street. As they came closer, the group of us being checked in just stood together quietly and watched. They smiled and said hello and greeted us. I was surprised no one approached them to speak with them as they talked amongst themselves. In this group was David Wells of the TV show Most Haunted. He was accompanied by his friend Norie. Psychic Fiona Broome from Hollowhill.com, one of he oldest and most respected websites about the paranormal was there, and she was talking to a young man with spiky blonde hair and eyeliner. He too was psychic and his name was Gavin Cromwell.

A bus pulled up and the door opened. A man climbed off. There he was, the man I had been listening to on the internet radio. I walked right up to him, stuck my hand out for him to shake and said with a big smile " Hi, I am Lesley Marden, I messaged you on MySpace." He recognized me straight away and somehow knew that I was a long time listener of his show. I hadn't told him that, but that is how he introduced me to his partner Maureen as she climbed off the bus. It was a fantastic day already, and it hadn't even started.

The tour started off with lunch. I met some lovely people that I sat with at the same table that was way in the back of the long room that we were placed in. As we waited for our lunch, we got acquainted and shared how we all came to be aware of the trip we were on. As we were talking, Ron was making his way through the room, saying hello to the people in attendance.

When he arrived at our table he said hello to everyone and then started to talk directly to me. He said "I am so glad I got to meet you today, I was really looking forward to it. I've seen you on MySpace and I see what you are doing on there." I replied that I was indeed on MySpace far too often and I wasted way too much time on there." He then said "Well, I just wanted you to know that I really am glad I got to meet you, and really, thank you for coming." He excused himself by smiling and telling us he had to get back to his table. He looked back and looked at me and again said "Thanks". The gentleman at my table said "It seems Ron was pleased to meet you". I really couldn't imagine why. I have to say though, I was extremely flattered.

On the way back to the bus I happened to be walking just behind David Wells. He was talking to a gentleman about his being originally from Scotland. I introduced myself and told him of my recent trip to Scotland and how beautiful the country was.

He asked what places and which castles I had visited. He said "No doubt Mary Queen of Scots had visited each, and was held captive in every one." and he laughed. Then I told him of that particular castle, where I had the experience of bursting into tears and how I couldn't explain it. He said, very matter of fact, "Past life, that is definitely past life." "Wow", I thought to myself.

I didn't offer up much else about myself. I kept pretty quiet about my experiences as they happened to me on the tour, except if someone asked. Like in the graveyard, I told Ron I could feel energy traveling up my leg, and when David asked if anyone had experienced anything at the Portsmouth Lighthouse, I offered that I felt very sad and lonely as we were walking the length of shoreline as we approached the Keeper's House. He agreed with me.

At Fort Constitution Gavin asked if anyone felt any energy where we were standing, and I told him that I was attracted to the Sally Port on the left hand side of the fort. Other than that, I kept quiet. I wasn't quite ready to let go of my vow that I had made when I was a teen. I just enjoyed being with these great people, and listened to their impressions. I savored every minute of the tour. People here were not laughing or doubting the impressions of the psychics that were being told.

Sally port, Fort Constitution

At the Bug Light, in South Portland, Maine, there was not much for the psychics to report so they made themselves available for the guests to chat with them or people could explore the area. I took the opportunity to talk with Maureen. She took the time to answer all of my questions about how she handles being a Trance Medium, and how she allows and doesn't allow spirits to enter her body. I asked if she could turn her ability on or off when she didn't want to use it and how she did that. She told me of some very frightening happenings and I listened and soaked in the information. I did not tell her any of my experiences that I had had in the past. I was there to learn.

When we arrived at the Portland Head Lighthouse, David was exploring a back room in the keeper's house picking up on the spirit energy of a boy. Fiona was talking to a group and giving her impressions of what she felt in the front room of the Keepers house, and Ron was in the next room by himself with his pendulum spinning ridiculously in circles and his EMF meter going crazy. He to said to someone "Get Maureen, get Maureen!" Maureen arrived and asked him some questions, and began to breathe differently and closed her eyes.

I switched my camera to "movie" and started filming her, apparently having a heart attack. She was channeling the Keeper of the Light house who had died and was he angry and in pain. Ron asked him questions and spoke to him through Maureen. The Keeper said that he Had given his life to the service and he wasn't ready to go. I was worried that Maureen was suffering while this was going on. The pain displayed on her face belonged to the keeper, but could her body and organs be affected by it?

As she came out of it you could plainly see that it had taken a toll on her physically. It took her quite a while to recover. I had never seen anything like that before. It wasn't like you see actors being possessed in movies. You could tell that this was not acting. You could also see the bond between Ron and Maureen, as Ron was right there to help her. I was amazed at her talent and in awe of her knowledge.

On the bus ride to our final destination, Ron asked Fiona to stand up and tell us about herself and she told us of an experience she had as a little girl. She was an eloquent speaker and told us how she saw the ghost of a worker in a hotel that her parents would vacation at in the summer. That was her first ghost. She told us she followed the ghost woman up to an attic where the woman had vanished.

As she stood at the front of the bus, I was taken with how intelligent she was. I didn't know it as I sat there in my seat on the bus, but luckily, this would not be the last time I would have the pleasure of being in the company of Fiona Broome.

We got off at our final stop at the Old York Cemetery in York, Maine before being dropped back off at the parking garage and bus stop where our tour began. We explored the graveyard and we all had the opportunity to take pictures together with Ron, Maureen and the psychic guests. Fiona seemed a bit surprised when I asked if she would mind if I had my picture taken with her. She kindly obliged and I thanked her. I thought to myself. "What a nice lady."

What an absolutely great day I had. I enjoyed every single minute. A light bulb went off inside my head and I decided right then and there that this was my thing, what I would do just for me from now on. This was what made me happy and it just felt like it fit. The difference was that before today, things just happened to me. This was the day I found the enjoyment of using what I can do purposefully, seeking out and embracing my gift of being able to touch the spirit world.

———

I found myself signing up for more and more tours and public investigations. With this positive first experience of being with like minded people, I slowly opened up to a certain few that I trusted and started sharing what I personally experience psychically with others. With each new experience and new adventure, the more I learned about what is out there, and about myself.

On one night I attended an investigation hosted by the NEGP at The Inn on Washington Square in Salem, MA. We were split up into three groups. Ron led one group, Maureen the second, and Ron's son, Ron Jr. led the third group. Each group explored a floor, and then we would shift so everyone could explore every floor in the house. At first I was a little disappointed that I would not be in Ron or Maureen's group, instead I was placed with Ron Jr. This turned out to be a blessing in disguise. As we walked the floors of the Inn, it gave me a new found confidence in my ability. I didn't have the crutch of having Maureen there to validate the psychic information I was receiving or to present the information before I had the chance to discover it myself.

I was aware of the spirit of a little boy on the third floor that I shared with my group, as well as the presence of a woman 2nd floor. She gave me the impression that she had a chest ailment, such as lung cancer or pneumonia, and my breathing seemed compromised. But, it was the visit to the Honeymoon Suite on the first floor that would prove to be the most interesting. Ron Jr. brought us downstairs to switch us with the group that was with his father in the Honeymoon Suite. It turns out, I was impressed with the younger Kolek. He was a very knowledgeable and pretty cool guy.

The charming room included a large four poster bed and a stone hearth fireplace and a Jacuzzi. Ron had set up a table for a glass divination session, where a glass is turned upside down and participants place one finger on the bottom of the overturned glass and communicate with spirits.

I stood on the side of the Jacuzzi and took some pictures. When Ron realized I was there he asked me to join in and lend a finger to the group gathered around the table. I placed my finger on the glass which was swirling around the table as Ron was asking questions.

Glass swirling, Inn at Washington Square, Salem, MA

It seemed that Ron had made contact with a young female spirit. When he asked a question, she would respond by moving the glass for yes. She revealed that she was afraid of a male spirit in the house who was very controlling. She seemed to be looking to Ron for protection from this spirit man who was bullying other spirits as well.

The glass suddenly stopped. When it started to move again, Ron pointed out that this time it had a different feel to it. It moved with more certainty than before. It was the spirit of the man. Ron asked him questions about why he was controlling the female and wanted to know why he was controlling. Apparently the man did not appreciate Ron's efforts to help the young spirit woman.

Suddenly Ron pulled his hand from the glass and stepped backward, as if something had moved him. He seemed to lose his breath for a moment. A member of the NEGP, Stacylynn, was standing next to him and exclaimed "Are you okay Ron? That was a warning! Are you alright?" He answered softly "Yes, uh yeah, I'm alright." He apparently had been struck in the stomach by an unseen force. After a moment, he gathered himself and decided to go on with the glass swirling. I took my finger off the glass and offered my space at the table so another one of the people in my group could have a turn. It then began moving again.

I was standing behind the circle of people at the table who had their fingers on the glass. Before I realized it, I found myself sitting on the edge of the Jacuzzi, with my hip pressed up against the wall. I noticed that my mood was changing. As I sat, I began to stare at Ron. I noticed none of the other people in the room. My focus was totally on Ron and the words that were coming from his mouth.

As my attention zoomed in I became angry. With every passing moment I was becoming angrier. I felt as if I was growing from the inside and I no longer seemed to fit inside my skin. My fingers felt like they wanted to split through the their tips and grow longer. My cheek bones seemed to raise up on my face and my cheeks felt sunken in and gaunt. My tongue had grown too large, and filled my mouth uncomfortably.

I angrily stared at Ron as he was asking questions at the table. He was oblivious to the fact that with every question he posed, my head was answering him with a slow nod yes or deliberately slow no. I have no idea if the glass was moving on the table. I was looking straight at Ron and it wasn't until he took the glass off the table that I realized that I was a bystander in my own body.

It was time to wrap up so Ron asked the group to find their way back to our seats where we had started the evening. With that, I realized that I was somehow not totally in control of myself, and I don't quite remember standing up or walking across the darkened room, but I do remember when the light from the adjacent room illuminated my face as I approached the doorway.

The next thing I recall, as I was walking through the door, Maureen asked me "Are you okay?" With the sound of her voice I realized that my hands were at my face. I was a bit dazed when I answered "I'm fine, I'm fine." and found my way to my seat.

As Ron and Maureen stood in front of the crowd, I sat in my seat and began to shiver uncontrollably. "What the heck is going on" I said to myself as my teeth chattered and my entire body shook. I tried desperately not to be noticed, and luckily I wasn't. After a few minutes my body seemed to calm. My cheekbones ached and I felt physically drained.

When I had regained my composure, I was able to add to the discussion about what things the group and I encountered while exploring the other floors. When Ron and Maureen finished up the discussion of the evening's events and said goodnight, I got to Maureen as fast as I could and explained to her what had just happened. She reassured me that what I had just experienced was normal after having a "jump in".

Maureen is so good at explaining things. She told me that a spirit had actually entered my body and used up so much of my energy that my body had to compensate and build the energy levels back up. To do that my body automatically began to shiver and created energy for my body to replenish itself. On my drive home that night I noticed that my cheekbones still ached. They bothered me for a few days afterward too.

That experience seemed to trigger something within me. Since that fateful evening, my abilities seemed to become more acute. I was more "aware" in so many ways. I could feel more. For example, I could now stand in a room and feel that a birth had taken place in it. I could now stand on a piece of ground, and recognize if it was sacred, or if something once living was buried there. When my student was feeling poorly, instead of feeling his headache, I could now pinpoint where the headache was. These improved gifts would surely come in handy at the next events I was to attend.

⚜

One of my next adventures was at The Tenney Gate House in Haverhill, MA. This too was an event that was open to the public. I was pleased to be reacquainted with Gavin and Fiona, the psychics that I had met on the lighthouse tour. John Zaffis was also a headlining guest on this investigation.

Upon entering the building, I was aware that many different things had taken place in the house. I felt a heart attack, and a choking, two separate incidents, straight away. At this point I didn't know where or why, but would be able to sort that out as we went along. There seemed to be different energies in different parts of the house.

As usual, the guests were split up into three groups, one with each of the headlining guests who were in attendance. As we made our way through the parts of the house and the ruins of Greycourt Castle, located on the hill behind the gatehouse, we were encouraged to share what we were experiencing.

I decided that this time I would not keep quiet, and share every bit of information that I was getting. It was such a liberating experience to share the impressions that I was seeing in my head and experiencing with my body out into the open. What was even better, was that when I spoke, people were receptive to what I had to share. No one doubted me and the Psychics who were leading our group confirmed my findings and my feelings.

Ah! Validation! There is absolutely no better feeling in the world for someone who was told all their life that these things were just imagination and lies. With every new excursion I attended, the more experience I was getting, and the more confidence I was building. I found that I was feeling a sense of fulfillment that I had never felt before.

At GhoStock 7 in Salem, MA, I became even more bold. I attended the three day event, held at the historic Hawthorne Hotel, with the hopes of learning from the experience of the featured guests, as well as supporting the book launch of a lovely woman whom I met on my paranormal path. I first had met Marley Gibson in the Ghost Chronicles chat room, then in person on a public investigation that she had attended with the NEGP. She attended investigations to research for the book she was writing. While doing research for her book, Marley became a very good ghost hunter herself. Marley's book launch for Ghost Huntress; The Awakening, was the first event slated to kick off the conference.

I was delighted to see many people whom I had met in attendance, as well as some whom I had met that were headlining the event. It was a very informative and fun conference where I learned a lot. The climax to the weekend was a ghost hunt where we could choose one of many investigations of haunted locations around Salem to be led by the headlining guests.

Forever Salem, Salem, MA

I chose to investigate Haunted Salem. A gift shop that was once used as a place where dead bodies were dressed and hair and make up were applied for funerals. I had heard that there may be poltergeist activity in the building. That was something that I had not yet experienced. John Zaffis and Father Andrew Calder, the two "big guns" of Demonology were leading this investigation. I couldn't imagine being more comforted knowing that if their was going to be poltergeist activity, I was with two extremely experienced men who had personally been involved with actual Exorcisms. They, of all people, would be prepared of any action we may encounter.

Upon entering the building, it seemed like a normal place, but the further back into the store you traveled, the thicker the atmosphere got. With every step down the stairs, that were located at the back of the store, I was aware that we were getting closer and closer to the source of the uncomfortable feeling.

Lesley Marden

Investigation, Forever Salem, Photo credit: Evie Haile

At the end of the hall there was an office. The employees were so afraid of this room that they never turned the lights off. Not even during the day. There were reports of coats flying off the coat rack in the corner and things being thrown across the room. As people sat at the desk they could hear scratching sounds behind them, scraping slowly down the length of the wall.

Father Calder got out his Ovilus and Mr. Zaffis plugged in his Shack Hack. The Ovilus is an electronic device created by Bill Chapel. It has pre recorded words in it's memory bank. Somehow, spirits can manipulate the device and by using the word bank can change electronic impulses into audible speech. No one knows exactly how it works. I have seen the Ovilus use words that are not even in the word bank, such as swears or the names of people in the room.

The Shack Hack is a Radio Shack transistor radio that has been altered so that the radio scans through all of the stations constantly. As the stations cycle through, all you hear is static and clicking. When you ask a spirit a question, it can pull any of the millions of words being spoken on any frequency that is transmitting a signal to answer your question.

We did hear some scraping on the wall, and we did pick up a few hits on the equipment. At one point the Ovilus moved slightly about the table like a planchette of a Ouija Board. One thing that was interesting, is that when the Ovilus was active, the Shack Hack was quiet, and when the Shack Hack had activity, the Ovilus was quiet.

Ovilus moving like a planchette, Forever Salem

After over an hour, I ventured upstairs to the store. There was a group of people sitting around in a circle on the floor with the Shack Hack. They were asking questions and not getting much of anything for a response. I noticed that as I was standing in front of the cash register, I couldn't stand still. My body was swaying back and forth and I was unable to control it. I was told that due to the high EMF (electromagnetic fields), I had to discount this "symptom". It has been show that where high EMF is present, people can get dizzy.

I wandered toward the group sitting at the front of the store, and I stood by the front door. I stood outside of their circle as a spectator, just listening. Then, there was some activity with the Shack Hack. I couldn't make out what it was saying, and the group on the floor had different suggestions as to what it might be saying. Whatever it was, something was trying to communicate.

As I watched, my left ear began to "tap, tap, tap", as if someone was poking my eardrum with their fingertip. I ignored it for a few moments, thinking I may be coming down with a head cold. "Tap, tap, tap." "Tap, tap, tap, tap". Finally I said to the circle on the floor "Something is tapping my eardrum and I don't know why." I then became aware of an older gentleman standing in front of me to the right a bit. I couldn't see him with my eyes, but I knew he was there.

Just then, the group on the floor had asked a question, and the Shack Hack answered them in such a way that two women on the floor recognized the information to be for them. The two asked another question, about their mother who was sickly and being cared for in a nursing home. The box answered them with a month and a number. It was the date of their parent's anniversary.

"Tap, tap, tap, tap" the sound in my ear was persistent. I started to get images in my head. I said to the women "Your father has passed?" They nodded. "Did he have a hearing problem?" They answered yes. That explained the eardrum. "Was he in the Armed Forces?" I asked as I was seeing a big cannon like gun in my head. The women answered that he had been at the Battle of the Bulge.

I do not know much about history, as I had mentioned before, so the words "Battle of the Bulge" really had no meaning for me. Then I asked if he was an Artilleryman in this war. They answered yes. The man showed me his hearing aids. I asked "Is this what led to your father's hearing disability?" "Yes" they said, "He came home from the war with barely any hearing at all."

As the man stood next to me I could see his grey hair and that he was wearing glasses. He then made me aware of his baseball type cap. It didn't have a baseball team logo on it, but was of that style. He was lifting it up off of his head and adjusting it by putting the back of the cap on his head first and pulling it down onto his head in the front. As he was doing this, I noticed that my left hand was making the same motion, as if I was wearing and adjusting the cap. I said to the women "He liked to wear baseball type hats didn't he." They smiled and said he always wore one.

I told the women that he wanted them to know that he would be there to receive their mother when she passed. As I relayed the message the women seemed relieved and happy to get this information. Then it dawned on me, Oh my gosh! I had just given them information from the other side! That was the very first time I had ever done that. Holy Cow! I did that!

Never in my wildest dreams did I ever think that I would be giving messages to people from the spirit world, but there it was. It just came naturally, and I didn't feel awkward at all. For a lack of a more elegant way to describe what I had just experienced, I would say that it was the truth. I was just speaking the truth.

Shortly after I had given the women their message from their father, there was a loud audible sigh that the people who were sitting on my side of the room heard loud and clear. Luckily one of the Digital Voice Recorders had captured it and we could bring it back as evidence. Other EVPs were captured as well during that evening's investigation. All in all it was a great night.

Edith Wharton House, Lenox, MA

The Edith Wharton House, known as The Mount, in Lennox, Massachusetts was the next adventure on the list. It was great to again run into so may people whom I had met on my past investigations, as well as meeting some new.

Before the nights events were kicked off and people were mulling about, Fiona Broome asked me if I would venture into the next room and view a painting that she found to be very interesting. It was a large oil painting that was hung on a wall in the dining room. It had darkened over the years and I had to really look at it to see the animals that were hidden away in the shadows on the canvas. One animal that seemed to stand out more than the others was a goat.

Energy emitting oil painting

Fiona asked me if I could feel the stream of energy that was being emitted from it. I could. As I repositioned myself in front of it I could feel the energy levels changing. When I got to a certain point off to the left side, I could feel a higher field of energy that seemed to be streaming from the painting. I said, "Oh, it is really strong here, Fiona, Stand in this spot". She agreed. I always have such fun with Fiona. She is such a gifted psychic, and such a brilliant woman. She is a wealth of knowledge and I am privileged to have been able to learn so much from her.

Just then I was distracted. I felt like something was watching us through the wall of French doors that led to the back field behind the house. I looked out. The light was just starting to fade outside as evening was setting in. My focus was drawn to the tree line that led to the wooded area beyond the field. I called over one of the other psychics in attendance and told him what I felt. He too could sense something in the woods, pacing from one side to the other, watching the house. I wondered if this was any indication of how the rest of the night would be.

The speakers were called to address the attendees and give their introductory talk before we were to be broken up into groups. The lights were turned off and the investigation started. My group had been designated to start on the first floor.

As we entered the Teddy Wharton room, I couldn't help myself from staring out the window. It had nothing to do with what had happened with the tree line before we started. The window had a view of a walled in piece of grassy area where there was a place to sit on marble benches. The group in the room behind me was asking questions and listening to the Ovilus. I was aware as to what was going on behind me, but I continued to just stare out the window. I thought of a man who was very depressed. As I touched the window casing I could see that a man did indeed spend a lot of time in this room and at this window.

As the session with the Ovilus continued, I stepped out of the room into Edith's Library. The shelved walls were filled with first edition volumes of books that she collected. Her original desk and chair sat there in the middle of the room. The room was cordoned off. How I longed to step over the barricade and run my fingers along the spines of the leather bound books and sit in her chair. I wanted to peek inside her desk to see if there were any pens or trinkets left behind.

Edith's desk. Note the bottom right window.
There seems to be a ghostly face of a dog.

Since I was unable to touch anything, I snapped some photos. As I do with every picture I take, I previewed each frame to see if anything obviously out of place shows up. I didn't notice anything out of the ordinary.

Our group was brought upstairs and we were allowed to split into smaller groups and explore. As Fiona and I took a step to go down the darkened hallway, we both experienced the strangest thing. As if we were watching a special effect in a movie, the hallway seemed to stretch out, further away from us, becoming longer to walk down. We both stopped dead in our tracks in disbelief and looked at each other. I put my fingertips together and pulled them out away from each other as if I were stretching handfuls of taffy and said "mmmyyyeeeeeooooowwwww" to express what I had just seen. Fiona too had experienced the exact same thing. How bizarre! I wouldn't have believed it if I hadn't actually witnessed it.

Movie effects hallway

In the bedrooms we experienced seeing shadows moving, and Fiona could hear Edith speaking condescendingly in French. Unexplainably, with every room we entered, both Fiona and I were immediately drawn to the windows. Here we were in this beautiful mansion, and I spent most of the evening looking outside.

Our group was gathered together and was sent to the carriage house. Downstairs as we entered the barn type structure, there was absolutely nothing going on. It was a very benign, quiet area with no energies, no sounds, no feelings. Upstairs, well, that is another story.

In the top of the barn area there was a lot of energy. I could see in my mind men working, and a little boy mulling about as well. There was about 15 in our group, and some were still downstairs and some of us were upstairs.

One man, Tom, was trying out his new microphone/recording gadget. He placed it down in the hallway that led to some very interesting rooms, then he came back into the barn area. He was behind me and he turned to go back into the hall when we heard this loud exhale. Tom said "Did you hear that? It was right here!" As he said that he held his hands in the area in front of his own face.

He couldn't believe what had just happened. "Did you hear that? Did you hear that?" he asked again. When he realized that he had left his gadget down the hallway, far enough away that it would not be able to pick up the noise, he was disappointed. He didn't have his proof, he didn't catch the evidence. What he did have was a room full of witnesses. Everyone standing near us clearly heard the disembodied breath. Tom still talks about it to this day.

After the excitement of that passed, I was curious as to what might be underneath us on the first floor, as it was not part of the downstairs that we could access from the way we were brought in. I went downstairs with a young man, whom I had met on previous investigations, and we found the original horse stalls complete with decorative iron bars at the tops.

A movie started in my head. I could see men walking busily, doing chores. Then I was aware of a male energy in the room. I pointed to where the spirit was walking and which direction he was moving and talked about the clothes he was wearing and what he looked like. The young man I was with seemed to be a little unnerved by this information. I asked him if he wanted to go back, as I noticed how close he was standing and that he was clutching my shirt. He quickly decided that would be a good idea, so we went back upstairs and rejoined our group.

Most of the group had left to make their way back to the house, to assemble for the evenings wrap up discussion. I hadn't explored the rooms down the hallway, so I asked two of my psychic friends to stay with me so I could check them out. We went through them one by one, each of us giving our impressions as we walked.

We then came to a room that I was a little apprehensive to go in. My friend Chris said "Don't go in there. I can feel Ouija from a mile away, and that room has definitely had Ouija played in it." I took some pictures from outside the room by sticking my camera inside the door. As we stood and talked, the atmosphere in the hallway seemed to be changing and Chris said "It's time to go." We all could sense a male energy becoming stronger and Chris had once had a jump in as well, but his experience was not a good one at all. He had a feeling that this male energy was going to try to do just that, jump in.

The Ouija room

We decided to leave. I was the last one to enter the stairwell and I could feel the male energy behind me. It was following us down the stairs. When I passed through the front door, Chris quickly closed it behind me and made sure it was latched. He placed his hand upon the door and said a prayer under his breath. He seemed very relieved to be out and he told me the prayer was to make sure the spirit would stay in the building and to protect us from it.

Well, these examples of my experiences with the paranormal should give you a good idea of what my life has been like. I have since gone on to being a member of private investigation teams, as well as working as a medium on public investigations. I have also found great joy in helping others by bringing them information about their loved ones who have passed that surround them and watch over them.

Through all of these adventures, I am still just a mom, a wife, a normal member of the staff at an elementary school. Most of my co-workers and friends still have no idea that I have done things like sit on The Old North Bridge at midnight with Richard Felix while he video taped himself singing a few verses of The British Grenadiers, hoping to attract some attention from the spirits of the American Soldiers that linger about. They have no clue that I can feel their heartburn, or their sore knee, or that I am aware of their grandmother standing behind them.

I am a normal person, who just happens to have some ability. I do not advertise or draw undue attention to myself. In fact, when people brag about themselves, about how intuitive they are, I watch them carefully. I am cautious as to what I say in front of them. I try not to judge, because I know how that feels. People have been misled in the past by those who make great claims, and I want you to be careful, so that you are not fooled too.

So, that is my story. I would like to thank all of the wonderful people whom I have met on my journey so far. I know that the road ahead will be as, if not more interesting than the past, as I learn something new with every day.

I would like to leave you with this. Please be kind to one another and treat everyone you meet with respect. A new day is dawning and people all over the world are becoming more aware of sprits and spirituality and how it all fits in with our daily existence here on Earth. There are spirits and angels around you everyday.

Live with love in your heart and a smile on your face and kindness in your touch. Accept yourself for who you are, and be accepting of others as well. Know that you are here for a reason, not by chance, and that you are loved.

Lesley Marden lives with her family in the beautiful Lakes Region of New Hampshire. As well as anything paranormal, Lesley loves photographing landscapes. She is happiest when she is helping others and very much enjoys working with children. Lesley is a certified Reiki Master and has worked as a Medium on private and public investigations.

facebook.com/lesley.marden

www.lesleymarden.com

Made in the USA
Lexington, KY
27 March 2014